Quality Counts
Achieving quality in social care services

Other SCA Co-publications

Residential Care: An International Reader
Meir Gottesman

The Children Act: A Social Care Guide
Ian Mallinson

Forthcoming:

Social Care: Rivers of Pain, Bridges of Hope
Leonard Davis

Creative Social Care
Doreen Elliott and Ronald G Walton

Stay at Home: Development and Decline of Schools for Young Offenders
Jim Hyland

Linkages: Networks in Social Care
Malcolm Payne

A Whiting & Birch Ltd / SCA Co-Publication

QUALITY COUNTS

Achieving quality in social care services

DES KELLY

and

BRIDGET WARR

Whiting & Birch Ltd
London
MCMXCII

Published by Whiting & Birch Ltd, PO Box 872, Forest Hill, London SE23 3HL.England.
USA: Paul & Company, Publishers Consortium Inc, PO Box 442, Concord, MA 017422.

British Library Cataloguing in Publication Data.
A CIP catalogue record is available from the British Library.

ISBN 1 871177 20 0 (cased)
ISBN 1 871177 21 9 (limp)

Printed in England by Short Run Press, Exeter

Contents

Foreword

THERE ARE some tasks which one addresses with pleasure; writing this foreword presents me with such an occasion.

In order to place developments in perspective, most of us require to relate them to specific events. 'Quality of care', 'good quality work', and 'a search after quality' are all phrases which seem to me to have been in current usage for many years within social care environments. 'Quality assurance', 'quality circles and cycles', and 'quality management systems' are phrases of a more recent time. My specific time event, is the publication of the Wagner Report in 1988, *A Positive Choice*. The essence of this report was the confirmation that living in a residential setting should arise as a result of choice, and that life in such a residential setting must offer a high quality of life opportunities; the report identified how such quality might be achieved. Choice without quality was, and still is, unacceptable.

The post-Wagner Development Group recognised the need to pursue this theme of quality, and one of four Working Groups set up to monitor and stimulate action following publication was given the title 'Aspects of Quality in Residential Care' Sub-Group. I have chaired this working group in reviewing the principles and components of quality of care, and in seeking to promote high standards of service. Since then, there has been a variety of useful publications, such as *Homes are for Living In* (published by HMSO for the Department of Health), and some very valuable research into how quality of life options are offered and secured.

The preparation and publication of *Quality Counts* fits well into this background. It brings together a host of good writers; the subject matter is dealt with in sufficient depth to leave the reader in no doubt of the principle but with an appetite for even more detailed reading; it addresses 'quality in social care' from a wide variety of perspectives and experiences.

I believe this book will become essential reading for all who work in social care settings, and who share the objective of offering quality of life opportunities. Most of all, it is readable. I commend it to you with pleasure and no fear of your disappointment.

Ian D Baillie
Director of Social Work
Church of Scotland Board of Social Responsibility

Preface

QUALITY COUNTS has been written at a time of rapid changes and developments within social care services. Every aspect of service has been touched with the rhetoric which promises a new order of things; from referral and assessment, the balance of needs and choice, partnership and participation. Structurally and organisationally the shape of services are altering, the composition of services across statutory agencies, the private and voluntary sectors are shifting. It seems like change, change and yet more change. In the midst of these forces *quality* has come to represent a constant about which there can be a level of agreement which sets aside differences in emphasis and style. Quality in social care services is a sort of rallying point when all around the sands are constantly shifting.

In this book social care is used as a shorthand phrase to include domiciliary, day, residential and community care provision across all sectors and for all user groups. There are overlaps with other welfare services such as health care and some of the discussion draws on examples in these sectors. The change which is being experienced for all involved in social care services - users and other stakeholders, practitioners and managers, trainers, planners and policy-makers - is fundamental and will set a course for future service development. *Quality Counts* describes the main themes of importance in the emergence of quality assurance in social care. It does not assume that elements of quality did not exist before we had the labels to define it or the methodology to measure it. However our understanding is developing and this book is a snapshot in a period of substantial change. It is intended to be an introduction to the concepts surrounding quality in social care and the many definitions it embraces. We have sought to include the main themes of the user view, of training and staff development, management, as well as the framework of standards and structures, the processes of inspecting, monitoring and evaluating, and wider perspectives such as Total Quality Management (TQM) and developments from outside the UK.

A major message of *Quality Counts* is that quality is everyone's responsibility. As a contribution to the continuing debate within social care, the emphasis throughout is on implications for practice.

Des Kelly and Bridget Warr

1

What is meant by quality in social care?

Bridget Warr and Des Kelly

THE EMERGENCE OF QUALITY IN SOCIAL CARE

SOCIAL CARE is an area of work in which the quality of service is of paramount importance. The provision of residential and day care services, social work and other community services by Local Authorities, the voluntary and private sector involving, as it does, a responsibility to people with special needs carries a clear requirement for the identification and maintenance of quality. Quality assurance is therefore a major and significant development in this field.

The pursuit of quality in services has been evident since the beginning of organised services, but the systematic approach to defining, evaluating, maintaining and improving quality is relatively new. Industry and commerce have already recognised the need for definable quality. People involved in the provision of social care services have much to gain from the experiences of industry and commerce - learning from their successes and false starts and developing further those aspects which apply most effectively to social care. To this can be added new techniques and systems to enhance the quality of services and thereby the quality of life of the service users.

It can be argued that traditional social care services have often been characterised by the combination of attitudes expressed as 'good enough', 'take it or leave it' or 'we know what's best for you'. The notions of choice, consumer satisfaction or 'consumer as sovereign' have been conspicuously absent.

Of course this is a simplistic view of the way in which the variety of services which represent social care have been provided. It is inevitably a generalised account of practices which have continued because of the disempowering effects of oppression and vulnerability on users, as well as the resistance to change on the part of the bureaucracies which make up the service providers. As a consequence even the best efforts at innovation or the commitment and dedication of social care practitioners has proved insufficient to mitigate these effects. Times are changing and quality is now firmly on the social care agenda. The quest for quality is being driven by several forces - political, organisational, economic - and most significantly by the demands and expectations of service users. It is likely that the combined force for change will prove powerful and there is already evidence that social care agencies are responding to the challenges.

THE CHALLENGES OF CHANGE

The need for more 'open' responsive services, tailored to the needs of users as customers, coupled with an attitudinal and cultural change on the part of staff and management is being recognised. Service providers are recognising the need for a disciplined and systematic approach to quality in social care services. With these developments come ever-increasing expectations of the services from customers, staff, the government and society as a whole. The need for a total organisational commitment to quality and its monitoring and enhancement is therefore clear.

Recent legislation (in particular the NHS and Community Care Act 1990 and the Children Act 1989) pay specific attention to issues of quality in service provision and build on the work started by the Audit Commission (1986) and the Griffiths Report on Community Care (1988), Home Life (Centre for Policy on Ageing, 1984) and the Wagner Committee (National Institute for Social Work,

1988), on residential services. The Wagner Development Group and the Department of Health's *Caring in Homes* initiative have also included a focus of assuring quality in service provision. In addition the Social Services Inspectorate series of publications *Caring for Quality* have contributed to the setting and safeguarding of standards in social care, including *Guidance on Standards in Residential Homes* (DoH, 1990), *Inspecting for Quality* (DoH, 1991) and so on.

Debate within the profession has been characterised by the outpouring of articles on quality in the social care press. The impetus to concentrate on quality in social care service provision is great and growing. And yet, despite the fact that the question of quality has become a particular focus of discussion in relation to the planning, organisation, delivery and evaluation of social care services, it remains a somewhat elusive and paradoxical concept. The notion of quality, in terms of definition and measurement, seems both simple and complex. At its simplest, quality is about meeting agreed individual needs, for example:

- a minibus which arrives on time to transport users safely to the local Social Education Centre;
- the provision of a clean single bedroom in a residential establishment; or
- the provision of genuine choice on aspects of living to service users such as flexibility on the timing of meals.

These examples each contain 'indicators' of quality which can be measured and about which judgments can be made. The time for meals or the arrival of transport are easily measured, it is the inferred judgment of quality about the way in which the service is actually provided which is more difficult. In this sense quality is experienced differently by different people.

Amidst all the complexity of deciding what is quality in social care, of measuring and monitoring, and evaluating outcomes, there is one certainty. *Quality in social care services is of paramount importance.*

The contributors to this book have variously addressed a wide range of aspects of quality assurance and the contribution of such support systems as staff development and training, management, and standards to the overall quality assurance picture. The chapters demonstrate a variety of approaches which the reader may wish to develop in relation to services in which she or he is involved.

SOME DEFINITIONS OF QUALITY IN SOCIAL CARE

Like all new developments, quality assurance has attracted its own jargon which is now applied widely, but not always in a helpful way. A word or phrase can mean significantly different things to different people and, therefore, every endeavour must be made to avoid jargon which obscures meaning.

Some of the words which may be used in any discussion of quality assurance are: quality control, quality circles, loops and teams, quality audits, inspections, evaluations, quality indicators, and standards. The need for common definitions is simply to facilitate communication. There is no need to seek one comprehensive and standardised system of quality assurance and it could be said that where this has been tried the result is often inflexible and unimaginative, which in itself militates against effectiveness.

British Standard 4778 deals with definitions of some of the vocabulary. For instance:

> **Quality**: 'The totality of features and characteristics of a product or service that bear on its ability to satisfy stated or implied needs'.

People involved in the Total Quality Management (TQM) movement (see Chapter 10) have variously defined quality as conformance to specification; meeting requirements or specifications; delighting the customer; zero defects; getting it right first time; continuous improvement; meeting customer needs; and excellence.

Some common patterns are emerging in the way continuous improvement is sought and terminology is arising from these improvements. Recognition of the need to involve service users (people with a direct and legitimate interest in the service), practitioners, managers and stakeholders in the pursuit of quality has led to the introduction of meetings, discussion groups, committees, taskforces and teams, containing representatives of each of these interests and described variously, according to their task, as quality circles, quality groups, quality action teams or quality improvement teams. Such groupings have a potentially high impact on the effectiveness of quality assurance and are seen by many as of fundamental importance.

A number of people in the social care field have fallen into the trap of equating 'inspection' with 'quality assurance'. As this book demonstrates, quality assurance is a much wider approach based on the continuing need to monitor and enhance quality. Inspection, whilst important, represents only a part of a quality control function which, in turn, is but a small part of quality assurance (see Chapter 5). The wider aspects of quality assurance must include the systematic identification of the purpose and aspirations of the service, of what constitutes quality in that service and how it will be recognised and monitored. In addition the standards which apply and the wide range of tools which can be used to plan and implement enhanced quality on a dynamic and continuing basis.

Such tasks could rightly be claimed to be the function of good management; quality is not an 'ivory tower' specialism of quality assurance teams. Quality assurance teams are not even a prerequisite of establishing effective quality assurance systems in an organisation. They do, however, have the advantage of introducing a degree of independence, the opportunity of providing support to line managers and of taking responsibility for defining systems and methodologies which will enable a significantly speedier introduction of quality assurance across an organisation. *They do not carry exclusive responsibility for the quality of services* and it is crucial that this is recognised by all. Responsibility for quality rests with each and every member of staff or volunteer and is the first responsibility of every manager.

Commitment should be demonstrated from the most 'senior' people - chief executives, directors and elected members - at all times. The commitment will be demonstrated not only through behaviour and attitudes (although these are of fundamental importance and relevance) but also through the establishment of clear public statements about the organisation's purpose, aims and objectives and its commitment to quality.

For instance, a number of social care agencies have:

- published their 'mission' or statement of values and principles;
- defined their aims and objectives on an organisational and individual service basis;
- adopted quality statements and a quality assurance policy;
- identified and stated standards and quality indicators for their services;
- devised and introduced proper complaints' resolution procedures which genuinely ensure an independent investigation and settlement without the risk of victimisation;
- established appropriate support, training, appraisal and development systems for staff and managers;
- linked the inspection function with a broader development approach;

and are still exploring ways towards greater quality. Many other agencies in social care, however, have only a few pieces of this jigsaw in place.

CONSUMER INVOLVEMENT

In order to define and monitor the quality of services effectively, providers must first acknowledge the primary importance of the wishes, needs and aspirations of the users of those services and of the other customers. Every service and activity undertaken in the social care field has its customers. Residential and social work services will have, among others, the direct recipients of the services, sometimes those people's families and, in the case of the voluntary and private sector, the sponsoring Local Authorities. A secretarial service has 'internal' customers and a Senior Management Team has the staff reporting to its members and the Board (or elected councillors) as customers as well as those people who use or purchase services.

A starting point for defining quality within each service should therefore be to seek the views of the customers. They are the final judges of what constitutes quality in their services and managers who ignore their views are compromising quality. The views of practitioners, other stakeholders and managers should also be sought and taken into account when defining quality and establishing standards. The use of quality action teams or groups may prove to be the most effective method in the definition and monitoring of quality as well as in the pursuit of continuous quality improvement. More detailed discussion of defining standards and involving staff and customers in the enhancement of quality will be found particularly in Chapters 4 and 10.

QUALITY DOCUMENTATION

The standards which determine quality in social care should be drawn up and regularly reviewed with close reference to the aims and objectives of the specific service which, in turn, should be entirely in line with and contributing to the achievement of the organisation's mission. A fuller discussion of an approach to setting standards can be found in Chapter 4.

Setting effective and relevant standards in social care has proved to be a more complex process than many had anticipated. A number of agencies have opted to set comprehensive minimum standards centrally and apply them to all appropriate services. This is probably the easiest and quickest way of completing the task, but it runs a real risk of discouraging improvement initiatives and of proving to be (in part at least) quite irrelevant to the customers of an individual service.

Many practitioners would state that in the continuum of inputs, process, outputs, and outcomes of any service it is the outcome which matters most and the outcomes which should, therefore, be subject to measurement. This is, however, problematical. Outcomes (the end result of the receipt of the service) are undoubtedly of paramount importance, but the problems of setting standards for them come on two fronts. Firstly, how can the outcome be evaluated? Even if it were possible (which it might be) to measure such outcomes as the degree of happiness, functioning, communication and so on within a family to enable such evaluation to take place, is that an inappropriate intrusion into personal privacy? The second problem is that such an approach undervalues the importance of the process and outputs aspects of a service.

A comprehensive set of quality documentation including standards, objectives, aims and strategic plan will provide the only sound basis for the continuous monitoring and improvement of quality. The terminology may differ but this is not important, provided those concerned understand the purpose of each document. Thus some agencies will have a 'Mission Statement' while others may prefer a 'Statement of Principles' or may divide the information about their reasons for existence from their framework of aims and guiding values and give each a different title. The important aspect is that the contents of such documents are clear, comprehensive, accurate and have been widely debated with 'customers' and staff.

The Quality Policy is a useful statement of the organisation's commitment to quality. It should contain a general definition of quality which can be 'owned' by all management, staff and customers. This may prove difficult to achieve but the process of definition, discussion and consultation is, in itself, useful. As experience grows and the organisation's practice develops, a revision of the policy should be undertaken.

The Spastics Society's Quality Assurance Policy, incorporating the Quality Statement reads:

> All activities undertaken and services provided by The Spastics Society will be of Quality.
>
> Quality means:
>
> - designed to meet the defined needs and preferences of service users and customers

- based on respect, openness and honesty
- staffed by people with a high standard of professional knowledge and practice skill, demonstrating commitment, initiative and flair
- sensitive and responsive to changing needs
- having clear aims, objectives and standards of service delivery, which are frequently reviewed and which are in line with The Spastics Society's Mission Statement
- effective and efficient
- continuously monitored, evaluated and developed
- regarded highly by service users and other customers.

No discussion of quality documentation is complete without a word about its accessibility. A written document, particularly a lengthy or obtusely worded one will not be truly accessible to every one concerned. It may be impossible to guarantee complete access, but it is clear that the contents will remain a mystery to many key people unless strenuous and genuine efforts are made to publicise them. Such attempts could include wide distribution, attractive presentation, opportunities for discussion, audio-tape recordings, video presentations with signed interpretation, large print versions, and straightforward and brief executive summaries. Unless all staff and all customers are appraised of the contents the likelihood of the organisation genuinely providing services of quality is very significantly reduced.

MONITORING

Monitoring is an important and integral part of good management. The inspection function has a part to play here, but should not be confused with the routine day-to-day monitoring, a responsibility which rests with management.

Effective monitoring depends upon the identification of those aspects of the service which give a real indication of its quality (as defined by the standards and quality policy). It is facilitated by good management information systems which ensure accurate and timely data being readily available and it is incomplete without a significant input from the users of the service and other customers. Such an input can of course be achieved in a number of ways, including through residents' committees, questionnaires, quality teams, quality action groups, formal and informal interviews, suggestion boxes, and the monitoring of the complaints resolution procedures.

It would be unrealistic to assume that all service 'customers' would readily participate in such activities, particularly where consultation and genuine valuing of their views by staff has not been part of the service culture. It is imperative, however, that support and assistance is given to ensure that they can, in time, participate fully or make a free and informed choice not to participate. Chapter 8 explores the issues surrounding the involvement of service users more fully.

The results of monitoring should be publicised among stakeholders and should be used as a basis for further improvements in quality and development of the service.

INSPECTION

Chapter 5 deals in detail with the issues surrounding inspection. There is a significant role for inspection and evaluation of services as an audit of quality but it is a specific role and does not, in itself, enhance quality.

Inspection most frequently concentrates on the inputs and processes of a service and, to some extent, on outputs (the immediate 'results' of the inputs and process). It is much harder to inspect or evaluate the longer term outcomes, which many would argue is what really matters in terms of service quality. For instance, an inspector can obtain from available data the 'inputs' to a service including, for example, number of staff and their qualification and experience, type and state of any buildings involved, unit costs, and details of catering arrangements. The inspector can observe the processes, including number and duration of individual contacts between staff and service users, the provision and content of meals, medicine distribution, punctuality of staff, and involvement of users in decision-making. Outputs can also be 'observed', such as behaviour (reflecting attitudes) of staff, users' degree of satisfaction with aspects of the service, ambience and atmosphere, and cleanliness of physical accommodation. The inspector cannot, however, be confident of systematically evaluating the outcomes (in other words whether the service users lead happier and more fulfilled lives as a result of access to that service), whether they play a full part in the opportunities and responsibilities of life in society, and whether they truly have equality of opportunity. Evaluation of outputs, processes and inputs should be informed by the overall effectiveness of any service in terms of the outcomes.

This is an area which needs further thought, clarification and development. At present there are many obstacles to be overcome and a number of approaches being explored. The development of methods of inspecting and evaluating inputs, processes and outputs is further advanced, and although further refinement is required, important issues are being highlighted.

Approaches to inspection vary within the UK, from the allocation of some 15 working hours for one Inspector to undertake data collection, observation, interviews, report drafting and presentation, to some 12 working days for each of four to six members of a multidisciplinary team to undertake an in-depth evaluation of a similar service.

A thorough inspection with a particular emphasis on the views of service users can be a trigger to enhancing quality. On the assumption that the systems to enhance and assure quality, mentioned earlier in this chapter and expanded throughout the book, are in place, the inspection should be a useful and accurate 'snap-shot' evaluation, from a team of people independent of the service itself and of its line management.

STAFF SUPPORT AND DEVELOPMENT

An important aspect of the assurance of quality is the valuing and development of staff. Recruitment and retention policies and practice which ensure the most appropriate appointments and minimise the loss of good staff should be backed by appraisal, reward and training systems which ensure that staff members give of their best and achieve maximal satisfaction from work. A quality assurance system which encourages staff members to take responsibility for (and pride in) the quality of their service will ultimately be maximising quality. The object is to prevent rather than merely detect bad practice and to encourage initiative and 'flair' which can so often be the stimulus to significant quality improvement.

The 'costs' of quality in any organisation and initial discussion of the need for quality assurance may draw a cynical comment about it being a luxury which cannot be afforded. This is a singularly short-sighted view - a fact about which this book should leave the reader in no doubt.

Drawing on quality assurance in commercial concerns for guidance, the cost of quality (in cash terms) may include any direct expenditure, such as the employment of staff dedicated to quality assurance and their costs. The costs of making other staff available to concentrate on quality issues, for instance through membership of a quality action group or similar activity, are debatable since this must surely be seen as integral to their work.

A form of cost-benefit analysis would, however, show clearly that the cost of *not* adopting quality assurance in social care is very much greater. In financial terms, the absence of quality assurance will mean a lack of established efficiency and effectiveness in service delivery, a loss of confidence on the part of stakeholders and, in particular, customers. This would, in turn, result (for the voluntary and private sectors at least) in a loss of 'business' and ultimately a loss of service.

The other effects of a lack of quality assurance are, however, equally devastating. A failure to pay proper attention to monitoring and improving quality undermines the values and principles of quality services. It leads to managers and staff being unclear about the purpose and aims of the service or to a failure to work systematically towards the achievement of those aims. This, in turn, leads to low staff morale and confusion and uncertainty about expectations of staff. Staff morale and functioning has a fundamental impact on the quality of the service.

SUMMARY

Quality assurance affects every aspect of the work of social care agencies and is inextricably bound up with Personnel, Management, Equal Opportunities, and other policies and practices. The key is the ordered and systematic approach and the genuine and continuous involvement of service users, practitioners, managers and other stakeholders. The following chapters look in more detail at the issues raised here to help with agencies' efforts to develop quality assurance systems and to enhance quality in social care services.

REFERENCES

Audit Commission (1986). *Making a Reality of Community Care.* London: HMSO.

Centre for Policy on Ageing (1984). *Home Life: A Code of Practice for Residential Care.* London: CPA.

Department of Health (1990). *Caring for Quality: Guidance on Standards for Residential Homes for Elderly People.* London: HMSO.

Department of Health (1991). *Inspecting for Quality: Guidance on Practice for Inspection Units in Social Services Departments and Other Agencies. Principles, Issues and Recommendations.* London: HMSO.

Department of Health and Department of Social Security (1988). *Community Care: An Agenda for Action*. Chair, R. Griffiths. London: HMSO.

Department of Health & Department of Social Security (1989). *Caring for People: Community Care in the Next Decade and Beyond*. Cmnd 849. London: HMSO.

National Institute for Social Work (1988). *Residential Care: A Positive Choice.* Report of the Independent Review of Residential Care. Chaired by Gillian Wagner. London: HMSO.

Oakland, J.S. (1989). *Total Quality Management.* Oxford: Heinemann.

2

Approaches to quality systems

Hugh Dunnachie

This chapter considers the processes involved in introducing quality assurance and quality systems to a social care agency. This involves recognising, defining and systematising the existing quality effort in an organisation, followed by the addition of new tools, techniques and insights into the existing practices to generate a fully functioning and coherent quality system.

QUALITY SYSTEM as used in this chapter is a system which involves all personnel at every level in the organisation, of effective resource allocation, management, supervision and practice which affects the quality of outcomes or end products of a service (Rutherford, 1989). The system should know when the organisation has achieved its prescribed quality targets and tell the organisation in a structured way, so that the information generated can be used to further improve service quality.

The approach described here is based on the author's experience of implementing quality assurance in a Local Authority Social Services Department. As a model it is applicable to other organisations involved in the delivery of quality social care and itself draws on research and knowledge gleaned both from service and manufacturing industry.

WHAT IS QUALITY?

Dictionary definitions of 'quality' have at their core terms like 'degree of excellence, relative nature or kind or character' (Concise Oxford Dictionary, 1985) and usually go on to equate quality with high rank or greater standing.

In its most general connotation therefore, quality is seen as being value orientated. Quality is not absolute, it is always expressed as a relative term - 'A is of better quality than B'. The BSI definition (BSI Handbook 22, 1990) in British Standard 4778 offers a more useful definition as a starting point when it describes quality as 'The totality of features and characteristics of a product or service that bear on its ability to satisfy stated or implied needs'. This last phrase very clearly indicates that quality is also judged on the customers' perception of how a service or product meet their needs.

The work of David Garvin of Harvard University (Garvin, 1984) has been particularly helpful in addressing the complexity of quality and helping to unravel its significance in social care. When it is said that '*this* service is of higher quality than *that* service' what factors are being taken into account when this judgement is made? Garvin identified five major approaches:

The transcendent approach A ccording to this approach, quality is synonymous with 'innate excellence'. This approach could also be called the 'aesthetic approach' in that it measures quality in the way that a work of art may be evaluated. Quality becomes an unanalysable property of a service (or a painting) which is judged after prolonged exposure to a variety of services (or works of art). This view is not so far removed from a lot of the judgements made about social care. Staff and users all form judgements about services which may, on the surface, appear identical in most respects. However, our 'sixth sense' tells us that there is a 'certain something' that makes one of higher quality than the other. This feeling may be definable in other terms after analysis and introspection, but on many occasions we are talking about something that we cannot take apart and unravel.

The product-based approach This approach to quality suggests that more of some ingredient makes quality better. For example high quality chocolate has more cocoa solids and so on. In social care it might be said 'give us more staff and we will do a higher quality job'. However, as Garvin points, out, not everyone has the same preferences or ranking scale and it is not the case that higher and higher staffing levels deliver a higher quality service to the users, whose level of satisfaction may be in inverse proportion to the number of staff involved in their care.

The user-based approach This starts from the premise, referred to above, that quality 'lies in the eyes of the beholder'. The highest quality service or product is that which best meets the user's needs. In social care, a responsiveness to user needs is clearly a high priority but, as in product manufacture, there are varying individual preferences that are difficult to aggregate and address. Furthermore, only a brief consideration of the question 'who are your customers?' leads to enormous difficulty in building quality into services when users/residents, their relatives and the public may have opposing views of their needs.

The manufacturing-based approach This approach sees quality as 'conformance to requirements'; fault free; right first time' (Crosby, 1979). Here quality depends on services meeting specifications which are tightly monitored in the attempt to deliver fault free services first time, and thereafter. In the new world of purchasing and providing, this model has direct applicability to social care. Purchasers will judge quality on the degree to which providers conform to specifications drawn up between the parties to the agreement. Quality here loses the value-laden messages of the dictionary definition - a mini is a quality car if you wanted a mini; a Rolls Royce is a quality car if that's the car you specified. If the purchaser received the service they specified, they received a quality service.

The value-based approach Garvin's final approach defines quality in terms of costs and prices, where quality is judged on conformance to requirements *at an acceptable cost.* This is clearly applicable in social care where agencies have budgetary constraints on what they may deliver and where officers and members alike must decide (often in public) to limit their requirements and often move from being 'excellent' to being 'average'. Their 'acceptable costs' feedback into their requirements.

This multi-definitional approach covers most, if not all, of the definitions of quality and illustrates how definitions from manufacturing have applicability to social care. One consequence of a multi-definitional approach is to illustrate why there is often disagreement on quality and in judging it. If, at any one time, the individuals involved have one or several approaches in their mind, it is small wonder that it is hard to agree. The disagreements may reflect the position of the individual in the process (e.g. service user, provider, purchaser, inspector, monitor, elected member) or personal knowledge, preference or background. However, amidst all this potential disagreement on quality there are characteristics of services (social care or elsewhere) that have a strong correlation with users' perception of quality.

SERVICE QUALITY AS USERS SEE IT

Research undertaken in the 1980s at the University of Texas (Parasuraman *et al.,* 1985) used information from retail banking, product repair and other service industries to identify ten determinants of service quality, all of which have direct parallels in social care. Different industries/ services may rank them in a different order, but consideration of all these factors will contribute to influencing consumer perception of quality. Most of these determinants cost nothing to install.

- *Reliability* Consistency of performance and dependability. You keep your promises.
- *Responsiveness* You respond quickly and creatively to customer need.
- *Competence* You have the required skills and knowledge to perform the service.
- *Access* You are approachable, convenient and easy to contact. People do not have to wait a long time.

- *Courtesy* You are polite and friendly as are your first-contact personnel.
- *Communication* You tell your users what is going on in jargon-free terms. You also listen and handle problems.
- *Credibility* You are honest and trustworthy and have the user's best interests at heart.
- *Security* You offer the service in an environment where risk is managed appropriately. You observe confidentiality.
- *Understanding* You make an effort to understand the user's specific needs and give them individual attention - no stereotyping.
- *Tangibles* The physical environment and the physical aspects of your relationship (e.g. written communication, your appearance) are consistent with the quality of your service. Users will perceive your professional services as inferior if your environment, manner and appearance are of poor presentation.

The researchers concluded the following:

- Quality is judged on whether our experiences tally with our expectations. If we get what we expect, we generally regard the experience as satisfactory.
- Quality is about process as well as outcome. The user of social care services may not agree with the worker on the outcome of their interaction, but if handled with courtesy, understanding and so on, will be more likely to have a satisfactory evaluation of the experience and return to the service. Remember the last time you had your car serviced and compare. Will you buy the same make again?
- Quality is often judged on how 'problems' are handled. When something exceptional happens, opinion-forming experiences abound. For example, British Airways evaluated customer satisfaction and found that satisfaction levels were higher in travellers who lost their baggage and were handled well than in those that never lost it.
- When problems arise a low contact firm/organisation

becomes high contact. This is crucial in managing customer satisfaction levels and in keeping loyalty.

How complaints are handled is crucial in industry and in social care. If purchasers and users feel that they are not being dealt with quickly and fairly, they will not wish to purchase again. This is another cost of poor quality.
Key points from this consideration of quality are given below:

- Service quality is about delivering services that are *fit for their agreed purpose* and *conform to requirements*.
- *Requirements* are a synthesis of the requirements of many stakeholders in the processes of social care but the user's requirements are paramount.
- Requirements may mean a *specification* that forms part of a block contract. It can mean an *individual agreement* for a care plan for one person.
- *Quality* will be judged on how the service delivered conforms.
- *Quality* services are *right first time*. Procedures which take mission, values and standards and turn them into *action* are critical in achieving this.
- Quality services are *designed* to be *fault free*: a *proactive* and *preventative* activity. Quality is not just about reaction, checking and detective work. *You cannot inspect quality into a service.*
- *Quality assurance* is all about achieving the above goals when designing quality services and a *Quality System* describes the process through which we guarantee we are delivering, reviewing and re-evaluating the promised service.

WHAT IS QUALITY ASSURANCE?

In the author's experience the two most useful definitions of quality assurance in social care are:

> An umbrella term for a continuous process of organisational development and improvement, building on current strengths and good practices, and

> using new tools and techniques to develop more systematic and disciplined methods of work.
>
> Øvretveit (1990)

and

> (aim to create)... a climate of innovation and development, in which staff feel motivated to assess the quality of their service and improve it - which involves everyone.
>
> Rutherford (1990)

These both relate closely to concepts from Total Quality Management (TQM, see Chapter 10) which at its simplest level refers to achieving quality at the lowest cost by harnessing everyone's commitment.

Certain key themes are expressed in these definitions.

- *Quality assurance is continuous.* You cannot say we have done quality and now we will go and do something else. It is a perpetual journey of improvement and innovation.
- *Quality assurance builds on current strengths.* Organisations already have ways of planning, monitoring, reviewing and evaluating services. They have targets, supervision and appraisal. All organisations have the basis of a quality system but it may need organising.
- *Quality assurance is part of good management* - just as much as financial, personnel, administrative and professional skills. Quality is everybody's business and, even if you have a quality assurance team, this in no way removes the manager's responsibility for quality assurance.
- *Quality assurance injects new tools and techniques.* Your quality assurance team or quality personnel should help you develop your professional and managerial skills so that you can plan, monitor and evaluate your performance and improve it in a systematic way.

The quest for *quality involves cultural change.* It is about the whole way that your organisation is run; everyone must be involved and committed from the very apex of the organisation downwards and across functional boundaries. It is pointless for care staff to commit to quality and quality improvement if they are not supported by their managers and by administrative personnel, *all* of whom have a key role in delivering a quality service. Figure 2.1 illustrates the differences between an 'ordinary' and a 'quality' organisation.

Fig. 2.1 The differences between an 'ordinary' organisation and one which provides a 'quality' service

Ordinary Organisation	**Quality Organisation**
Provider led	Customer led
Focus on detecting problems	Focus on preventing problems
Cost containment through cutting resources	Cost containment through a disciplined approach of matching resources available to service priorities
Values numbers	Values people
Low spending on training	High spending on training
Value about goals/roles /standards at any level	Explicit and disciplined about goals/roles/standards at all levels
Treats complaints as a nuisance	Treats complaints as an opportunity to learn
In awe of technology under management control	Uses technology selectively
Runs by systems	Runs by people working with people
Sees quality/service efficiency as separate endeavours	Relentless search for improvement of the organisation with quality/ service efficiency as indivisible elements
People do not know where they fit into the quality chain	Manages the quality chain

(Information by courtesy of The Capita Group, Brentford, Middsx, UK).

IMPLEMENTATION STRATEGIES FOR QUALITY ASSURANCE

The journey to quality and quality assurance requires a clear strategy for implementation within any organisation. This section draws on lessons learnt from the specific experience in the author's own organisation to illustrate a more general approach, highlighting key themes and target areas. All organisations are different and have different cultures, history, quality systems and management 'styles', hence there will be differences in the way that the drive towards quality is managed. However, the key steps remain essential and must be taken in any organisation truly committed to change.

Step 1: Organisational commitment

It is clear from all experience of quality assurance and total quality management that, if managers at the top of an organisation do not drive the quality assurance effort, it will fail. Senior managers must commit to quality and 'own' the strategy and the methodology.

Within social care agencies the model of quality assurance to be adopted will depend on the characteristics of the particular organisation. The development of the model may well start by officers in any or many parts of the organisation thinking about what quality and quality assurance mean for their service. However, at a fairly early stage in the research and development of this thinking, dialogue must be established with the key senior managers responsible for operational activities of the agency. These key managers have to lead others by example and through their actions demonstrate a commitment to change ways of thinking about doing the organisation's work.

Organisational commitment does not stop at the top and all staff have a part to play in the quality effort. Quality needs to be owned and driven by everyone in the organisation who, over time, will share in and actively contribute to the improvement of service quality. However, when you start, you must start at the top with a commitment to commencing the journey to quality.

Step 2: Review current practices

It is essential that the organisation reviews its current practices before establishing in more detail the approach to quality assurance. 'Current practices' mean the ways in which the organisation:

determines its values;
establishes its goals;
sets standards for performance;
monitors and measures performance;
reviews and evaluates;
feeds this information back; and
changes and improves its functioning.

In other words, audit the basic quality system. How, for instance, does the organisation address the questions: 'How well are we doing?'; or 'How do we know we are doing the right things?' The former question is about efficiency; the latter about effectiveness. 'How do we change things we want to improve?' is about quality improvement.

In looking at these fundamental issues in the organisation, there will emerge many positive elements. Certainly the organisation will discover a great deal of good practice already. Within social care agencies, many elements of a quality system may well already be in place:

mission statement;
service planning;
performance indicators;
standards of practice;
supervision and appraisal;
review;
staff development;
inspection and audit.

These elements may not all be highly developed in all agencies but they are not alien concepts. They may not be systematically interrelated as they should be, but their presence indicates a fertile grounding for the further development of a quality system.

A second positive of this process of establishing where you are, is that it involves staff in starting to look at quality and reinforces the message that they are already involved in quality assurance as an integral part of their practice. This is an essential step in engaging staff later on in the drive towards quality.

Step 3: Agree your approach to quality assurance

As indicated above, the stimulus to begin may be generated in various parts of the organisation. A statutory requirement to set up an inspection unit may lead to a consideration of a broad approach to quality. Alternatively, an organisation may recognise that its quality practices could and should be more systematic and seek to improve them in a coherent way, consistent with the experience of other industries and services. Wherever the organisation starts there comes a time when a particular model must be agreed (and to which the organisation must commit).

In saying this, it is essential to remember that the notions of quality and quality assurance are themselves developing and changing. Therefore, at first, it will only be a broad approach upon which the organisation must settle.

Step 4: Clarify roles and responsibilities

As stated above, the approach to quality assurance will depend on the nature of the organisation, the stimulus to change and other factors.

The approach adopted, therefore, to some extent determines the structural response to quality assurance. For example, a statutory organisation, required to set up an arms-length inspection unit may well decide to combine its quality assurance and inspection functions in the one unit. Another organisation might wish to extend the remit of its staff training and development section and have them act as enablers and facilitators of quality improvement. A non-statutory social care agency wishing to improve and systematise its quality effort may well set up a small team to both assist managers and staff and also carry out specific audit functions on behalf of senior management and so on.

Whatever model is chosen, it is essential that the roles of quality assurance professionals and managers are kept distinct and clear and that this is agreed and publicised in the organisation. Just because the organisation has a quality assurance team, this in no way removes responsibility for service quality from operational managers and staff. Quality is an integral part of good management and must remain so.

The quality assurance arm of the organisation is there to help managers systematise and direct their quality efforts by giving advice, knowledge, skills and new techniques. It may also be there to independently report on how the organisation is performing in its pursuit of quality.

Step 5: Raise the profile of quality assurance

By this stage any organisation should have committed to quality, decided its approach, clarified its current practices, and agreed roles and responsibilities. All this can have happened with comparatively little contact with front line staff, managers and service users. However, as total organisational commitment is essential, the profile of quality assurance must be raised.

In the author's authority the strategy involved both written publicity and personal contact with staff. Following agreement as to the approach and strategy, a high quality leaflet was produced on the authority's approach to quality. This was backed up by more general information in departmental publications that went to all staff.

The leaflet also formed an introduction and invitation to all front line managers to attend 'Roadshows' in geographical divisions in which the key concepts surrounding quality and quality assirance were introduced. These people and their immediate supervisors had been identified as key opinion leaders and as a starting point for contact with front line staff.

Aside from introducing concepts from quality assurance, the Roadshows also attempted to encourage managers to celebrate their existing good practice. They were able to clearly state some of the methods by which they were already assuring quality.

The Roadshows finished with an invitation to engage in projects with the quality assurance team. The aim of the projects was to get front line units to begin to use techniques from quality assurance to establish or fine-tune their quality system and to improve service delivery. Particularly popular were projects on user/customer surveys as staff were keen to develop the tools to plan jointly with users and find out more effectively how they were satisfying customer requirements. Projects were also undertaken on performance indicators, standard setting, review and evaluation and many others.

The key element in all these was that front line staff (and to some extent users) were quickly involved in thinking about quality and taking action. Secondly, they were helped by the quality assurance team to do this. It is essential that quality assurance personnel are visible, credible and active in the organisation's journey to quality. Cynicism and demoralisation are more likely to arise when the quality assurance personnel are invisible or merely regarded as purveyors of rhetoric from headquarters. The quality assurance team can no more afford to only get it 'right second time' than any other service provider. It must be 'right first time' otherwise the organisation has taken a step backwards in its pursuit of quality.

In local authorities it is also important that elected members are involved in the discussion of quality assurance. Seminars or workshops, outlining the key concepts and clarifying members' concerns and interests in quality, form both a useful dialogue per se when members need to evaluate the relationship between the cost and quality of services as well as addressing the issue of ownership of departmental standards of service.

Step 6: Establish an open system of communication

The next section fully explores the components of a quality system for any organisation, but prior to so doing it is important to stress that the system must thrive in an environment of open communication. In this instance, communication about quality.

Social care organisations already have well developed systems of communication. The information which feeds up, down and across has traditionally been management information related to finance, occupancy levels, personnel matters, some client information and so on.

Information from the quality system includes all this and more. By fully utilising existing methods and developing new links, information on how the agency is functioning can be shared widely. Also solutions to quality problems in one part of the organisation need to be spread to other parts of the organisation. There is a role here for quality assurance personnel in spreading the good news, but staff groups and management groups at all levels must gather and share information from the quality system and see to it that quality targets as well as financial and occupancy targets are set and monitored.

It is important to remember that performance on quality is so often good news, involving all staff in a concerted effort to work with users to improve service. This is at a time when other news and management information may be less encouraging. Getting it right first time motivates and inspires and there must exist multiple mechanisms to share this.

Furthermore, the Director or Senior Managers have the right to expect to easily answer the questions: 'How are we doing and how have we improved?' They have made the commitment to quality and legitimately expect a payoff in both improved performance and evidence of this in management information. This does not come overnight, but the quality system must produce information and inject it into the organisation's existing (or revised) communicating system.

QUALITY SYSTEMS

Step seven in implementing quality assurance should be the creation of a quality system using the existing elements in the organisation and changing, developing and improving them.

At the beginning of this chapter a quality system was referred to as: a system that involves all staff in effective resource allocation, management, supervision and practice which affects the quality of outcomes or end products of a service. In listing the components of a quality system, it will be seen that they inter-relate and are all mutually interdependent. This means that wherever you decide to start when you tackle the systematisation of your existing quality system, you will end up dealing with all the elements of the system. This will become more apparent as the quality system unfolds.

Key components of a quality system

Mission statement

There should be a written statement which defines the organisation's mission. This defines the fundamental reason for the organisation's existence, states its beliefs and responsibilities. It also details the general scope of its activities and defines the intended users. In simple terms it is the answer to the questions 'Why are we here and what are we here for?'

It is quite clear that teams within large organisations can and should have their own mission statements consistent with the overall general mission statement of the organisation as a whole. Mission statements are crucial (but often missing) because not only do they express the synthesis of the values and purposes of any unit but they also say what the unit is *not* for. The section below on the 'Cost of Quality' (p.33) refers in greater detail to the cost of doing the wrong work.

Missions will change as goals and objectives are met or as resources alter. They are, therefore, closely interwoven with 'political/resource' decisions and need regular review. This also reinforces the view that agencies or units must be flexible and be prepared to change their approach as both resources, priorities and their mission changes.

Statement of strategic goals and priorities

The organisation must say what activities it will undertake to achieve the mission. These strategic goals should be broken down into specific objectives which can be evaluated as to their attainment. In general the organisation must be clear about its strategic decisions and priorities, which are based upon the values expressed in its mission statement. The two processes must correlate. The activities undertaken to accomplish the mission are in effect the policies of the organisation. Policy, at its simplest, being what any organisation decides to do.

Service design, strategic planning and formulating procedures are therefore key parts of the quality system not only because they aim to match activities, priorities and mission but also because they should aim to get services 'right first time' by building in quality at the design stage. At an individual unit level the same applies in so far as goals and priorities should be agreed (consistent with the overarching organisation) which support the mission.

Standards

Organisations must, as part of their quality system, have criteria upon which performance can be judged. These are standards and describe the level of service to be achieved. Having decided the mission and priority activities a measurable level must be set to be monitored.

> **Example 1**
> An organisation might espouse the value: 'elderly people should be valued and respected'. This would be incorporated in the mission statement. The strategic objective that derives from this could be 'people in elderly persons homes should have personal space and privacy'. A standard related to this could then be : '80% single occupancy', i.e. a criterion upon which performance can be judged. The performance indicator is '% of single occupied rooms'.

Indicators

Performance indicators are the means by which an observer or investigator knows whether the standard is being achieved - they are the measures by which conformance to the required standard is evaluated. Other performance indicators could include waiting time, levels of customer satisfaction, levels of unallocated work, alternative meals available, numbers of daily activities offered.

Monitoring and documenting methods

Monitoring methods are the means by which an observer finds out about performance. The methodologies used to assess levels of attainment of standards will be dealt with in

Chapter 4 but will range from observation, questionnaires, spot checks, mystery customers through to self-reporting and other mechanisms. This does however stress the key message that having standards and indicators is meaningless unless you collect information on performance, and document and report the information.

Reporting system

The section on 'Strategies for Implementation' (p.22) dealt with communication systems - it is crucial that the information on achievement of standards (and on how problems have been solved) be communicated in a digestible format within the organisation. It is key management information and, in particular, is the basis for service review and evaluation. This information is at the heart of the process of knowing how well the organisation unit has achieved its objectives.

Review

Any quality system requires that there be a review procedure. In social care an individual care plan which states agreed objectives, required performance and monitoring methods and which is reviewed is itself a paradigm for a broader quality system. Review is a management tool for assembling the information on conformance to required standards (i.e. quality) and deciding whether this was achieved or not.

Evaluation

Evaluation is one step beyond review in that, if reviews answer the question 'Did we achieve what we set out to achieve?', evaluation asks 'Was our original objective the right one?/Did we choose the right target or plan?'.

Both review and evaluation are essential parts of the quality system and need to feed back documented information into the quality system at the top (Figure 2.2).

Quality improvement techniques

Review and evaluation are often seen as occasional 'events' rather than as the continuous process which they really are.

Fig. 2.2 Quality system

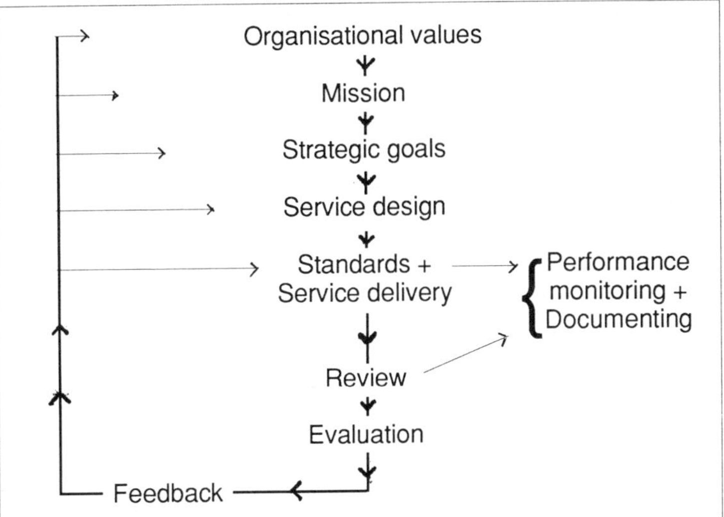

The ever shortening horizontal arrows on the left indicate the reducing degree of impact of evaluation as you get further from service delivery. Evaluation seems more likely to impact on standards rather than on the overall mission.

In a manufacturing context performance is continually monitored and reviewed and subtle adjustments or improvements are made. In social care services reviews and evaluations often tell managers about problems or issues that the staff and users already know about and would have liked to have tackled.

In a quality system there must exist opportunities for staff and users to participate in the identification and solution of quality problems. Quality assurance offers new tools and techniques to harness the creative energies of all staff and users to systematically improve their service, often improving cost effectiveness.

A quality action team of staff and users set up to identify and solve such problems is an effective technique in any setting and requires little or no outside facilitation.

Similarly, quality circles, small voluntary groups who meet regularly to improve the quality of service and propose solutions to quality problems, may well prove highly

> **Example 2**
> The staff of a day centre for elderly people in a rural area had identified two major problems:
> (a) the time of the minibus journey for the users; and
> (b) the high petrol costs.
> The staff and users jointly identified the problem as, in part, relating to unnecessary journeys to pick up users who were unable to attend and who had rung in after the minibus had left on the collection round (it was a two hour journey).
> The solution suggested: a mobile phone in the minibus, which enabled the driver to revise the route dependent on which users were available.
> This solution paid for itself and more very quickly and enhanced the quality of life for the users by reducing journey time. It was then shared with other units as a quality improvement scheme.

effective in getting staff fully involved in quality improvement (Robson, 1989).

Techniques that help staff 'stand in the shoes' of the users, such as 'customer profiling' are also useful in improving service quality. Customer profiling (Foster *et al*, 1990) which involves staff in identifying critical incidents or features of service quality and seeks to develop service standards to improve performance at these critical junctures, is an extremely useful technique in social care.

Whilst there are many and various quality improvement techniques which cannot be fully covered in this chapter, the key theme is that staff and users often know how to improve service quality. If enabled to do so by using systematic approaches to quality, the service to users and the morale and involvement of staff should improve dramatically.

BS 5750/IS0 9000

No chapter on quality and quality systems would be complete without reference to the above (see BSI Handbook, 1990). Whilst BS 5750/IS0 9000 does not prescribe standards, it does state the mechanics of organisational management to ensure that standards of service are delivered. BS 5750 gives a disciplined structuring of behaviour in order to obtain the desired results and offers a system of quality management and administration that, when fully complied with, ensures services are designed, enforced, reviewed and modified to meet requirements. It is a disciplined structured quality system that has been translated into social care and allied fields. I would question how high on an organisation's agenda this work should be when there are so many less time-consuming and costly activities in the quality assurance arena in which to engage to greater effect.

The Social Care Sub-Committee of the British Quality Association (BQA) has done considerable development work on the applicability of BS 5750 to social care and interested readers may wish to obtain more information from the BQA.

THE COST OF QUALITY

What about the cost of quality? Is it all worth it?

In the private sector, one of the most basic management problems is to strike a balance between the cost and value of quality assurance. Employers can get an accurate idea of the cost of employing quality assurance personnel but information on the values of quality assurance are harder to evaluate, ie. how much did poor quality/failure cost us?

Feigenbaum (1983) identified three major categories of costs of quality:

- appraisal costs
- prevention costs
- failure costs

He hypothesised that there is an optimum point (see Figure 2.3) where appraisal and prevention costs equalled failure costs. In social care appraisal costs might relate to costs associated with review, inspection, supervision and evaluation. Prevention costs relate to service design, procedures, quality improvement schemes and systems that are organised to 'get it right first time'.

Failure costs might include:

- time wasted getting information
- time wasted doing the wrong work
- not knowing what customers require and doing the wrong work
- errors and mistakes
- duplication of work
- excessive complaints
- costs of redress
- poor reputation
- poor morale
- high absenteeism and staff turnover

These costs are potentially high in financial and human terms.

By investing in quality assurance, failure costs are diminished and services are made more effective. Appraisal and prevention pay off. Figure 2.3 illustrates Feigenbaum's (1983) hypothesis.

Fig. 2.3 The cost of quality

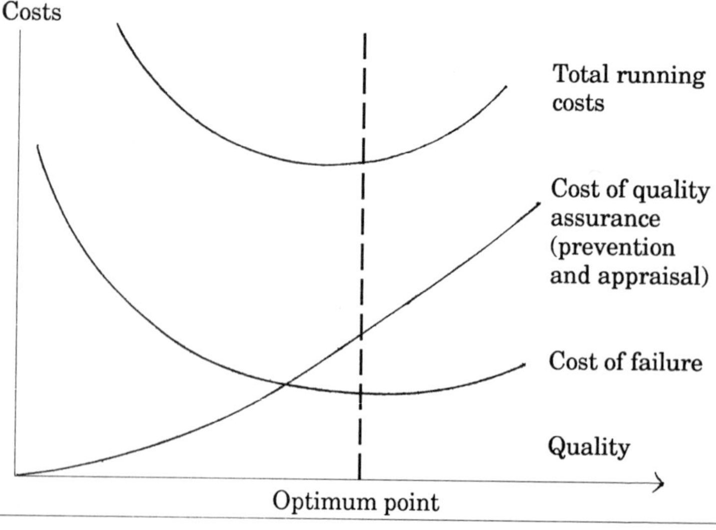

Whilst there may be some questions as to the applicability of a Feigenbaum-style analysis to social care, the basic premise that there is a trade off between investment in quality assurance and its pay off in terms of improved service effectiveness holds.

It is clearly the case that services with a clear mission, based on agreed values, delivering services at an agreed standard, subject to review and evaluation, and interfacing with service users, are likely to be more effective than those services drifting inertly along, changing incrementally and haphazardly. Similarly, prevention of the sort of failures and problems identified here by a clear commitment to total quality, involving everyone in a continuous process of innovation and development offers all involved in the social care field an opportunity to work together for improved services in the future.

So, yes, it is all worth it.

REFERENCES

Atkinson, P. (1990). *Creating Culture Change: The Key to Successful T.Q.M.* IFS.

British Standards Institute (1990). *BSI Handbook 22* (May).

Concise Oxford Dictionary (1985). Oxford University Press.

Crosby, P.B. (1979). *Quality is Free*. McGraw-Hill.

Feigenbaum, A.V. (1983). *Total Quality Control: Engineering and Management,* 3rd ed. McGraw-Hill.

Foster, M. *et al.* (1990). *Improving the Service Quality Chain: Managing Service Quality*. IFS.

Garvin, D.A. (1984). What does product quality really mean? *Sloan Management Review* (Autumn).

Øvretveit, J. (1990). *Managing Service Quality.* (unpublished lecture notes, March/April).

Parasuraman, A. *et al.* (1985). Quality counts in services too. *Business Horizons* (May/June).

Robson, M. (1989). *Quality Circles: A Practical Guide*. Gower.

Rutherford, J. (1989). *Quality Assurance and the Notion of Quality.* (unpublished paper).

Rutherford, J. (1990). *A Question of Quality.* (unpublished paper).

3

Quality and its social construction by managers in care service organisations

Ann James

Quality did not just fall out of the sky. Neither is it part of some great plot to rearrange the commission and provision of care services in the future. It is simply an idea ripe for its time. This chapter asks why and how quality arrived on the social care scene and how, as an idea, it is itself collecting meaning for people working in and around social care. It begins, therefore, to ask questions not just about what quality means to care service management, but why it is provoking both such enthusiasm and such cynicism among managers and practitioners.

The chapter draws on three sets of source material. Firstly, the quality literature itself, spawned largely by the private sector in business and commerce and by management consultants to that sector; secondly, organisational development literature both in its traditional form and the more recent contribution of the New Public Management (NPM) (Hood, 1991); and thirdly, a whole range of management development and consultancy interventions by the author within care service agencies over recent years. The latter includes a four-month project commissioned by the Department of Health Social Services Inspectorate to consider quality assurance in Social Services

Departments conducted in conjunction with a Social Services Inspectorate (SSI) Steering Group by the author in early 1991 (DoH, 1992). The use of this source material is not intended to imitate a research methodology. On the contrary, it is simply to bring a broad set of observations to bear upon the quality debate itself. Those observations are not presented to prove a point or seek affirmation; the intention is simply to provoke discussion around issues of quality. Above all they seek to distinguish between what quality is currently about from what it might be expected or intended to be about.

The nature of much of the source material means that this chapter draws on the experience of quality initiatives in social services. Transferability to other service sectors should be made with caution: one would expect that the process of constructing quality in other settings may well be similar in pattern, but that the form that construction takes will vary according to the specific character of the service involved.

The chapter begins by looking at how quality arrived on the social services scene, and suggests it came with a particular heritage which has influenced its progress. It then summarises the brief context into which the quality debate fell in the social services, and therefore the process by which quality came to be part of a solution, or, at the very least, part of a way of managing contemporary problems in social services. What appear to be the four major ways in which managers are using quality in social services are then considered. These are: as a set of tools; as a set of values; as a way of managing power and control in organisations; and as a way of managing change and innovation. It is suggested that these ways are not exclusive nor comprehensive, but important in that they suggest that quality, like any bright idea, can be hijacked for a range of purposes and can collect meaning. The chapter closes by suggesting what quality needs to be about.

THE HERITAGE OF QUALITY IN SOCIAL CARE SERVICES

IF QUALITY is an idea ripe for its time, its heritage, and the special nature of that heritage within social services, has informed the way in which it is currently being addressed.

That heritage began, for our purposes, in the Financial Management Initiative launched by The Treasury (House of Commons, 1983) as part of Mrs Thatcher's (the then Prime Minister) intention to create a civil service which would be, in that classic phrase, 'economic, efficient and effective' (the 3Es). As that intent extended into public services in general and local authority services in particular, it was advanced by the creation of the Audit Commission with the Local Government Finance Act, 1983, with which arrived the second classic phrase, 'value for money' (VFM). What that heritage demonstrates is that, from the beginning, financial, ideological and political imperatives were to be wrapped up together in what was later to emerge as quality.

This was picked up by the Audit Commission Report, *Making a Reality of Community Care* (Audit Commission, 1986) which highlighted perverse financial incentives within the system of provision for elderly people, and did so by the use of simple comparative statistics, or performance indicators. And so performance indicators emerged as tools for policy guidance as well as financial calculation (they had already existed for the purposes of financial calculation from the 1960s when social costs and benefits were embraced by central government departments). The Griffiths' Review of Community Care (DoH & DSS, 1988) and precursor to the White Paper, *Caring for People: Community Care in the Next Decade and Beyond* (DoH & DSS, 1989) in November 1989 drew attention to the ways in which complex and separate hierarchies and political processes worked against creating a seamless service for users. The White Paper identified, for the first time in Social Services, the notion of quality control as a way of achieving what it called a 'high standard of care'. What was emerging therefore was not just an intention to make VFM and the 3Es happen, but a series of mechanisms for achieving that; mechanisms which utilised information, accounting and quality control systems made possible through new technology.

These systems were not necessarily innovatory, however. Many of them were borrowed, more or less appropriately, from private sector manufacturing companies, with their emphasis on product design specification, and production for consumers rather than partnership with users in joint service activities. Indeed there was some criticism that the public sector was rapidly adopting accounting designs already proved inadequate in manufacturing, as evidenced by the downturn in manufacturing industry. We were learning to practise methods which professional accountants had themselves rejected (Humphrey, 1990).

Running parallel with this movement was a central and local government concern, reflected by the public, with 'scandals' particularly in the field of child abuse, and with it an increasing awareness that creating policy documentation did not necessarily result in policy implementation. This was most clearly evidenced in the Rochdale case of 1990-91 where, in spite of previous SSI recommendations, the court found policy and procedural guidelines seriously wanting.

An ongoing way of tackling what was seen as a problem of control from the centre was by the use of specific grants, in the Rochdale case designed to promote staff training in child abuse. To obtain the grant Departments had to begin to catalogue to SSI their intended and achieved performance in numerical form, a process which again took them down the performance indicator route.

In addition, the Wagner Report had generated a new interest in the outcomes of residential care and with it the creation of new agencies in the public and private sectors designed specifically to promote that interest. These organisations themselves began to produce literature on service outcomes and promote service training. Meanwhile the SSI was working on a number of other fronts: promoting managerial work in what became known as 'key indicators', offering professional guidance on standard setting (e.g. *Caring for Quality: Guidance on Standards for Residential Homes for Elderly People*, DoH, 1990), and promoting clarification over training requirements.

Alongside these initiatives Social Services Departments were themselves creating mechanisms to review performance at the individual, unit and departmental levels through systems of appraisal, inspection and planning, amongst others.

The central government decision to implement the requirement on Social Services Departments to set up Inspection Units from 1 April 1991 under the National Health Service and Community Care Act, 1990, in spite of delaying implementation of the Act as a whole, pushed many of these review processes into an inspectorial rather than quality mode. This is reflected in the guidance, *Inspecting for Quality*, issued by SSI for Departments (DoH, 1991).

In conclusion, the heritage of the quality movement in Social Services Departments is important in as far as it informs the approach currently being adopted. It is an approach as important for what it omits as for what it includes. As an approach it has four characteristics.

- It is top-down, driven essentially by financial, ideological and political imperatives.
- User views have had, as yet, very little impact on that approach.
- The approach has pre-empted the use of certain tools and mechanisms, such as performance indicators and cluster studies, facilitated by new technology.
- It has come at service quality through the route of quality control or inspection, and therefore to some extent represents a reactive rather than proactive approach, emphasising sanctions rather than incentives and control rather than motivation in the quality process.

The limitations of this overall approach have been recognised elsewhere, and there is evidence to suggest that user involvement and concern with service outcome will continue to lead to a more well-rounded view in the future (Barnes and Miller, 1988).

THE ORGANISATIONAL CONTEXT FOR QUALITY IN SOCIAL CARE SERVICES

In short, what is and has been happening to Social Services Departments in the late 1980s is that they are being asked to move away from a monopolist provider role to an enabler, purchaser and occasional provider role within a mixed economy of provision. At one level the debate about quality is a debate about the mechanisms to be used to make that shift. That shift is essentially politically and financially driven. What is being seen is the effect of short term and highly directed central government intervention designed to facilitate eventual central government withdrawal in favour of a self-subsistence economy largely dictated by the market and more recently softened under current Government policy to the notion of the social market. The process in the late 1980s mirrored almost exactly that used by the Government to withdraw investment from manufacturing industry in the late 1970s and early 1980s. It is displayed in its most advanced form in the early 1990s in the National Health Service (NHS), where leadership has already been divested to a Chief Executive and Management Executive and where the process of the internal market is intended to speed up the process of accountable management.

At another level the debate about quality reflects a very real concern as much within central government as outside it, with the nature and extent of services as provided to date. This concern has been amplified by real or calculated public mistrust of the social work profession as demonstrated by a number of 'scandals'.

Finally, the debate about quality successfully locks into a general desire to improve service quality as perceived by the service user or potential user. Given some real concern that consumerism is itself being co-opted by service professionals, there is no doubt that the general direction of *Caring for People* (DoH & DSS, 1989) his widely supported in its intention to create much more responsive and individualised services for users than that provided in recent years by a 'welfare state'.

In some ways, therefore, 'Quality' has taken over from

'Community Care' in being the generalised term of endearment which everyone can currently use without fear of offence. As such it has become one of several devices used in the management of change.

Organisations have responded to the requirement to change in predominantly four ways: they have become more business-like; they have restructured; they have planned ahead; and they have invested in people.

The 'Business Solution' takes many forms, but in essence it is a financial solution. It says get the bottom line right and everything else will follow. And, of course, it is correct. For if the bottom line is not right the Director gets sacked, or the members do not get re-elected and so on. So a good deal of energy is invested, and quite appropriately so, in the bottom line. That means unit costing, cash flow analysis, workforce planning, etc. It brings with it a whole technology of information systems, business language, culture and training. Part of that business solution represents part of the quality initiative, namely that part which promotes economy and efficiency. So, for example, we find the local committee (Social Services Committee, the Probation Committee, the Voluntary Sector Board) shifting from one of confirmation to one of policy maker and evaluator.

But of course getting the bottom line right, staying in business, is not the same as doing the business. What the business solution teaches is that certain beasts have to be fed in order to generate permission to be able to manage service procurement and provision. It dictates the parameters within which services are to be managed. What it does not necessarily do, and what needs to be done, is to determine how services are to be managed within those parameters. This is the other role for quality.

The restructuring solution is one still very much favoured by central and local government at the time of writing. One might argue that the public services legislation of the 1980s represents one massive attempt to resolve issues by restructuring. This solution has taken three major forms. Firstly, renegotiations between the centre and locality, usually around changed accountability, responsibility and authority relationships and probably using catchwords like decentralisation or budget delegation. These negotiations are essentially about redefining power relationships around who controls whom or what and who holds the mandate for that control. The problem in this situation is of course that restructuring itself has a destabilising effect such that power given away is often experienced as loss by the giver and dumping by the receiver.

The second most common form restructuring takes is change in the leadership. This ranges from, at its crudest, sacking the football manager (or Director of Social Services) to changing the nature and locus of executive decision-making as with NHS Trust status or the integration of Social Services and Housing within the local authority. Both represent a challenge to traditional professional leadership. Both imitate private sector behaviour.

Finally, restructuring can take the form of disaggregation by a variety of means. It might be with a big bang, as with the purchase/provider split in the NHS, or through the back door, as, for example, when homes for elderly persons take on trust status. It might use catchwords like partnership or the mixed economy, and be achieved through mechanisms like compulsory competitive tendering (CCT) or local management of schools (LMS).

If you cannot pay your way or restructure your way out of a problem, you might think of planning your way out of it. Management by Objectives, Cascade Planning and Business Plans are three popular forms being used locally to create Community Care Plans. As a technique for the centre to manage the locality or to generate information for future prediction, planning is extremely effective, and therefore much loved by central government departments and agency headquarters. Unfortunately as an operational management tool in a rapidly changing environment planning is often at best a guestimate, at worst a hostage to fortune. Whatever else management of social services has learned in the last ten years it is that planning is not to be confused with implementation. Writing a strategy is a far easier process than implementing it.

What seems to happen in management in practice is not the same process as that of planning. It is planners who set goals, strategies, guide implementation and review them. In a rapidly changing world managers seem to act first, review later, and often find the right plan only emerges with hindsight. The problem with this is of course that managers who have confused planning with managing think that if only they did it faster, trained harder or were clearer, they would get it right. And planners who have confused management with planning tend to agree with them. So managers create whole edifices of guilt and huge piles of blame in failing to see planning as only one part of the managerial process. Here quality can come in as one way of bringing together strategic planning and operational management around what appear to be neutral goals. Quality can act as an integrating device between centre and locality.

The fourth solution is investing in people. The management literature coyly talks about 'putting people first' but there is most certainly a growing trend, perhaps encouraged by depressing workforce analysis statistics, to regard people as being represented in a number of ways. Firstly, there is a new regard for training as represented by developing accreditation and exchange schemes. Secondly, organisations designed to represent non-professional 'people' interests are springing up (e.g. the Carers' Association). Thirdly, there is developing concern in a contract culture in working with boundary organisations across the private, public and voluntary divides. Fourthly, there continues to be major interest in creating cultural change within organisations. Here quality emerges as shorthand for the 'New Culture', which it is intended will find staff flexible and responsive to users.

Characteristic of the four responses to the changes being demanded in social services is that they are managerial in character. Moreover, their managerialism is not any managerialism but that of the new public management (NMP) (Hood, 1991). Characteristics of the new public management include entrepreneurship, financial accountability, decentralisation and disaggregation of service units, employment of new technology to control information on performance, competition for resources, pay and service contracts linked to performance, responsiveness to users and, finally, service quality. It might be suggested that quality may be being used as part of the cargo of the cult of the successful new public manager. Which brings us on to look at the four major ways managers are, at present, using quality within Social Services Departments: (i) as a set of tools; (ii) as a set of values; (iii) as a way of managing power and control in organisation; and (iv) as a way of managing change and innovation.

Quality as a set of tools

Over the decade of Thatcherism, central government declared the intention to work at best towards a free market in public service, at worst to an internal market or mixed economy. Central government also demonstrated, with housing, with education, with health and others including social services, the route to be taken to achieve that intention. There were four clear stages. Firstly, to clarify tasks and accountabilities; secondly, to set and maintain standards; thirdly, to introduce competition; and fourthly, to privatise or disaggregate by opting out mechanisms.

Clarifying tasks and accountabilities has taken a number of forms: these include legislation (such as The Children Act, 1989), policy and procedural guides, job descriptions, service agreements, and accountability statements. Setting and maintaining standards include the formation and maintenance of selected performance indicators, the utilisation of management information systems, staff appraisals, unit reviews and performance related pay (PRP). Introducing competition may include removing monopoly status as with compulsory competitive tendering, or direct funding to competitors, such as independent organisations. Finally, privatisation or disaggregation include opting out and trust status provisions.

The quality movement is central to these kinds of activities. One of the things quality does is to legitimate both the process and the end of moving towards a free market in welfare or, arguably, after the premiership of Margaret Thatcher, a social market. It does so simply because the concept of quality is apparently noncontroversial and feels good. Quality is apparently something every individual can identify with in their own job. It appears to bring broad and unmanageable ideas like 'the mixed economy' down to earth and converts them into activities that everyone can get on with everyday in their own way. To 'do' quality you do not need to see the whole vision (though it helps). What you need to see is quality in your own job.

Quality, therefore, becomes a set of tools, a means towards an end as yet unclear. It is a way of getting on with the job in a time of unprecedented change, when arguments about ends are very difficult. As such, quality is a very important integrating concept. To be used at this level quality needs to be grounded in the hardnosed detail of everyday life. It is what Persig calls 'the art of motorcycle maintenance' (Persig, 1974; 1989).

To achieve quality in this sense, staff need to know what is expected of them and how they are doing in relation to those expectations. They need to have quick, easy and personal access to that information. That information needs to be reliable and it needs to be credible. Staff also need to be properly trained to achieve the set level of expectation (and that includes cover for training to make sure it happens). The evidence is that staff, properly trained, able to influence standard-setting, and in control of information about their performance become their own most ardent critics. Moreover, they put pressure on line management to clarify accountabilities in the form of job descriptions, etc. (DoH, 1992).

An extended analysis of quality as a set of tools is given in DoH (1992).

Quality as a set of values

For some managers quality is a means to an unspecified end; for others quality is an end in itself. For some managers quality is hardnosed, utilising management information to match performance against pre-stated requirement. For others quality is value-added; it is that indefinable extra. Persig captures this difference when he talks about quality as Zen as well as the art of motorcycle maintenance (Persig, 1974; 1989).

In reality, of course, quality is not just about facts and figures, nor just about feelings and values. It is about the relationship between the two. It is about how values affect behaviours and practice and vice versa. Certainly the expression of quality needs to be captured in hardnosed data and experience in order to prove its existence at all. But that existence is by no means value-free. Being 'better' or being 'more effective' is a perjorative term. As such it makes assumptions about what being better or being more effective might look like. And there are certainly more than one set of assumptions about that.

Christopher Hood, for instance, suggests there are at least three sets of core values in public management: 'lean and purposeful', 'honest and fair' and 'robust and resilient' (Hood, 1991). He calls these three sets sigma, theta and lambda, which he sees as corresponding roughly to the management values used by Susan Strange in her account of the evaluation of different regions in the international sphere (Strange, 1988) and at least two of which correspond to Harmon and Mayer (1986) in their analysis of the narrative context of public sector organisation (see Fig. 3.1).

Hood suggests that the three different sets of values underpinning public services management result in different criteria for measuring success or failure, or effectiveness and non-effectiveness in 'managerialese', or quality and lack of quality in our terms.

Sigma-type values (lean and purposeful) stress the relationship between resources and objectives or goals to seek to minimalise wastage in that relationship. What this means in practice is that objectives and goals must be trimmed to be readily identifiable and achievable; activities must be highly specific and segmented in order to impact most effectively on set targets; and a technological infrastructure must exist to make the management of information possible. Hood illustrates sigma-type values in the use of 'Just-in-time' inventory control systems (or 'Just-too-late' in the UK?) and performance pay. One of the likely effects of such approaches is to make management an administrative activity, designed to coordinate and control highly divisionalised time management structures. Another

Fig. 3.1 Three sets of core values in public management

	Sigma-type values	Theta-type values	Lambda-type values
	KEEP IT LEAN PURPOSEFUL	KEEP IT HONEST AND FAIR	KEEP IT ROBUST AND RESILIENT
STANDARD OF SUCCESS	Frugality	Rectitude	Resilience
	(matching of resources to tasks tasks for given goals)	(achievement of fairness, mutuality, the proper discharge of duties)	(achievement of reliability, adaptivity, robustness)
STANDARD OF FAILURE	Waste	Malversation	Catastrophe
	(muddle, confusion, inefficiency),	(unfairness, bias, abuse of office)	(risk, breakdown, collapse)
CURRENCY OF SUCCESS AND FAILURE	Money and time (resource costs of producers and consumers)	Trust and entitlements (consent legitimacy, due process, political entitlements)	Security and survival (confidence, life and limb)
CONTROL EMPHASIS	Output	Process	Imput/Process
SLACK	Low	Medium	High
GOALS	Fixed/Single	Incompatible 'Double blind'	Emergent/ Multiple
INFORMATION	Costed, segmented (commercial assets)	Structured	Rich exchange, collective asset
COUPLING	Tight	Medium	Loose

from Hood, 1991. Reproduced with permission of Blackwell Publications, Oxford.)

is to make information the source of power and hence something to be withheld for trading purposes rather than given away.

In contrast, theta-type values (honest and fair) stress the pursuit of integrity and openness in public services. As such, not only are the objectives of theta-type systems likely to be multiple and even conflicting (depending on one's view of what is right), but there is likely to be more emphasis on the process by which decisions are reached, a process which includes multiple checks and balances. Examples of theta-value systems in operation include appointment by committee, appeals procedures and signature of letters. In theory, the employment of theta-type values should lead to open consultation and consensus. In practice and in a political environment such as local government, they are more likely to lead to irresolvable conflicts of value and competition for the moral high ground. As Michael Willson (1990) demonstrates, the development of the entrepreneurial manager and promotion of a risk-taking culture is at variance with the expression of theta values. Indeed, one of the double binds of the new public manager is that she or he is encouraged to operate creatively beyond the need for checks and balances, but penalised if things go wrong.

Finally, lambda-type values (robust and resilient) seek to promote survival, and therefore to reduce environmental and organisational uncertainty through a whole range of mechanisms including change reduction and the warehousing of additional resources. The objective of lambda-type organisations is to keep going against all the odds, and is the preferred management mode to reduce the need for crisis intervention.

For Hood, the success of a public service organisation is dependent upon how far it manages to accommodate all three sets of values and practice together. What Hood's discussion does is to identify how and why the debate about quality is around, and why quality is important within Social Services Departments at the present time.

It is a way of managing dissent over values which cannot themselves be resolved. Social Services, like all care service agencies, are essentially value driven in both the professional and political contexts. The headlong rush to the free market of the 1980s did not succeed in taking everyone along with it. Indeed, the pace of progress has varied both across and within organisations. It is no accident that Social Services and other public service organisations have picked up on the 'Excellence' literature (Peters and Waterman, 1982) with its emphasis on core values. It fitted very neatly with where those organisations saw themselves. Ironically, unlike in the private sector, public service organisations do not actually need reminding of values since they emerge in surfeit in just about every political and professional arena. What the 'Excellence' literature allowed some of these organisations to do was to indulge in a favourite occupation. That occupation was arguably self-indulgent since conflict over values can never be resolved but only converted into conflicts of interest.

What quality does, almost accidentally, is offer a value-base that everyone can appear to agree with and can feel good about. Quality is simply a social construct with meaning attached to it. So, for some, quality is about users; for others it is about staff performance; for others about information systems and task, and so on. Quality, like community care, is a generalised notion, a receptacle into which different meaning can be dropped by different people. It is everybody's distant cousin and nobody's baby. Hence, quality can be an integrating device and a communication device at times when integration and communication are difficult. Its value as such is therefore very important. Equally important, it can be a device for keeping people sufficiently apart, locked into their separate meanings, again like community care. How and why words collect meanings is by no means accidental. Quality can be a substitute for core values at a time when core values are up for grabs.

Quality as a way of managing power and control in organisations

Organisations are deemed to have lifecycles. Rapid changes in organisational mode results in chaos while the organisation either sorts itself out and emerges in a revised form, or collapses. Public organisations, by and large, have not been allowed to collapse. However, the level and speed of change being required of them to meet environmental requirements has and is resulting in an extended period of chaos which may or may or not turn out to be constructive. What the chaotic state does is allow a series of redistributions of power to take place, one of which will emerge as more robust than the rest and become the new form of organisation. Those redistributions of power may take several forms. They may be coalitions of people which emerge to take power at the expense of others, for example professionals, politicians or managers or groups within those rankings. They may be geographic, represented in arguments between centre and locality or locality and individual unit. Or they may be financial, represented in issues over budget delegation and authority.

Restructuring, decentralisation and budget and staffing delegation, though significant in their own right as meeting the requirements of the government agenda, are also part of a much broader debate about power and control and about how service organisations as a whole will emerge out of the changes now being required of them.

Quality is a small part of that debate and potentially a very constructive part of it in that it is one of a very few integrating notions and carries with it the potential to put users up front in creating new forms of organisation. The difficulty is, however, that quality can be identified with managerial control and can therefore be rejected by staff. Certainly there are very real and appropriate needs for managerial control over increasingly decentralised and disaggregated provider units. The problem is that many of the same mechanisms are used to promote quality as to effect managerial control (information systems, policy and procedural guides, review, inspection, appraisal, etc). It is all too easy therefore for managers to talk quality but mean control and for staff to hear quality but understand it as control. Given the heritage of quality in Social Services which links it with inspection, this is most likely the case. Given the organisational chaos described earlier, managers' use of control mechanisms may be interpreted quite appropriately by staff as power-seeking. The danger is of course that the baby will be thrown out with the bathwater; quality will be rejected as simply a control mechanism used by managers.

In addition, being able to promote a particular set of practices or a particular set of values is an expression of capturing power in organisations. Ownership of any new and powerful idea bestows power and status on the persons promoting that idea. The attachment of a specialist language enhances the superiority and exclusiveness of those having this power. This is so with quality, where the language of quality serves only to admit entrance to the inner sanctum. It is a language used almost exclusively by those whose jobs are in the business of quality and those who wish to join them. It serves therefore not to create a culture of quality but one of exclusiveness. Exclusiveness creates cynicism among the excluded such that quality, its expression and its language, is described as 'flavour of the month'. Thus the excluded deal with their exclusion by the use of put-downs.

This process is not exclusive to care service agencies. British Telecom, for example, distinguish between 'Quality Initiatives' and 'Operational Initiatives'. The difference between these two as activities is unclear. What is clear, however, is that quality initiatives seem to collect status and resources.

The labelling appears to reflect not the nature, level or function of the enterprise, but how well it has been marketed within the company and therefore whether or not it has managed to capture the status of a quality label. Quality appears to collect cargo and therefore is good to be part of. This labelling process can be a particular problem where quality has become associated with a particular status group in an organisation (such as the Quality Assurance Unit, or the Inspectorate), who are then seen as owning quality on behalf of the rest of the organisation. This, of course, lets everybody else off the hook. What it also does (and this is more subtle) is redefine quality to take on the existing characteristics of the dominant group who profess it. In this way quality can become culturally bound and can reproduce uniformity rather than variety. At its worst it can be a way of preserving the status quo by marginalising issues not of central concern to the dominant group (most notably equal opportunities). None of this behaviour is, however, particular to quality itself. It is rather about how organisations as a whole deal with new initiatives and absorb them into existing and well formed arrangements in order to maximise certainty.

Perhaps more distinctive to care service agencies is what appears to be the way in which quality is used to capture the power through capturing values. So quality, if it takes on the moral high ground is, like values, always something I have and you do not. More than this, quality, because it is often confused with excellence, can become perjorative. It then becomes ideal, unattainable, and less a managerial aid than a managerial obstruction. It simply demonstrates to people what they cannot do. As a result it can leave people demoralised and cynical, as indeed has happened with quality initiatives in Jaguar car manufacturers and in some parts of the National Health Service.

Quality as a way of managing change and innovation

Moving away from a monopolist provider role to that of enabler, procurer and maintainer requires very different kinds of organisations from those traditionally associated with large-scale care service agencies. Like the new public manager, so the new public service organisation is developing a number of key characteristics. It is flat rather than hierarchical; smaller rather than larger, with specific competencies rather than general wisdom; and with decentralised rather than centralised forms of resource allocation and accountability. It is built for flexibility rather than stability, and promotes innovation over security.

These kinds of characteristics do not as yet fit comfortably with notions of public accountability and service reliability. The problem is one of managing the transition. This is where the concept of quality can come in.

What the SSI study *Committed to Quality* (DoH, 1992) demonstrated was the power of quality to bring together those elements that needed to be brought together to achieve change and innovation across highly divisionalised and specialist line management function. Through quality initiatives the top manager was forced into dialogue with what can only be described as 'product champions', that is a number of charismatic senior operational managers who were obsessed with achieving high quality in their particular area. Through quality initiatives, Red Star or express systems of communication were set up to throw up 'starbursts' or examples of good practice and to bring these to the attention of line managers who were in turn pushed into acknowledgement, into linking such initiatives together and thereby generating motivation and enthusiasm for high achievement. Similarly, the creation of effective and fast information systems gave staff the capacity to comment upon their own performance. Quality assurance staff, much like the old Training Officer, were acting as 'mixers and fixers', passing learning across highly segmented organisations. Quality assurance initiatives allowed staff to step out of role for a moment and reflect on their job in relation to other parts of the organisation. In this respect the Quality Assurance Unit takes over the same function as research and development in the large firm, which according to Parritt (1991), not only operates as a major factor in implementing innovation, but also contributes to rethinking internal and external organisational boundaries. In a world where traditional wisdom is displaced through constant restructuring and staff mobility, mechanisms to communicate have to be found in order to create organisations that can learn. Parritt talks about learning by doing, learning by using, learning by failing, learning by studying and learning from competitors. What quality can do is bring back learning and institutionalise it into organisational life. In this way it is no different to effective staff development and, indeed, staff development might be regarded as one of its functions.

CONCLUSION

Management fashions come and go. Quality is an idea that is ripe for its time in Social Services; it is an idea that has already peaked in the National Health Service. For some it has become bogged down by its own time-consuming methods for standard-setting and standard-maintenance, associated less with success and achievement than with failure and cynicism. That is a considerable loss, for what quality represents is not just a set of tools which can be used to practice in an unconventional world; not just a set of values which can be drawn upon: but at its most simply, a way of talking to each other and practising across line management boundaries, across service boundaries, across organisational boundaries at a time when we need to be talking together and practising together.

The challenge for quality assurance in social services at the present time is to begin and continue those conversations and those joint practices. The challenge for the future, and a much more difficult one judging by experience in the NHS, British Telecom, British Airways and others, is to build in capability and capacity to renew quality initiatives in the long term. For quality assurance, underneath its conceptual preambulations, is about how to survive in the transition to a mixed economy of care. There is a very real sense in which quality appears, as yet, to have only a very peripheral relationship with service users. Yet if quality is a social construct, it can, one assumes, take on further meanings beyond those imposed by managers. To bring a very powerful concept and set of activities such as quality to the benefit of users would be to attach real meaning to it.

REFERENCES

Audit Commission (1986). *Making a Reality of Community Care*. London: HMSO.

Barnes, M. and Miller, N. (eds) (1988). Performance measurement in personal social services. *Research, Policy and Planning*, 6(2).

Department of Health (1990). *Caring for Quality: Guidance on Standards for Residential Homes for Elderly People*. London: HMSO.

Department of Health (1991). *Inspecting for Quality: Guidance on Practice for Inspection Units in Social Services Departments and Other Agencies. Principles, Issues and Recommendations*. London: HMSO.

Department of Health (1992). *Committed to Quality: Quality Assurance in Social Services Departments*. London: HMSO.

Department of Health and Department of Social Security (1988). *Community Care: An Agenda for Action*. Chair, R. Griffiths. London: HMSO.

Department of Health & Department of Social Security (1989). *Caring for People: Community Care in the Next Decade and Beyond*. Cmnd 849. London: HMSO.

Harmon, M. and Mayer, R. (1986). *Organisation Theory for Public Administrators.* Boston: Little, Brown.

Hood, C. (1991). A Public Management for all seasons? *Public Administration,* 69, pp.3-19.

House of Commons (1983). *Financial Management in Government Departments.* Cmnd 9058. London: HMSO.

Humphrey, C. (1990). Accountable management in the public sector. In *Issues in Management Accounting*, Ashton, D., Hopper, T. and Scapens, R. (eds). Prentice Hall.

Parritt, K. (1991). Key Characteristics of the large innovating firm. *British Journal of Management*, 2, pp.41-50.

Persig, R.M. (1974). *Zen and the Art of Motorcycle Maintenance* (reprinted 1989). Black Swan.

Peters, T.J. and Waterman, R.H. (1982). *In Search of Excellence: Lessons from America's Best-Run Companies.* New York: Harpen & Row.

Strange, S. (1988). *States and Markets: An Introduction to International Political Economy.* Pinter.

Willson, M. (1991). Contracting consumption. *Local Government Chronicle.*

4

Establishing standards in social care

Pete Ritchie

This chapter explores the place of standards in the development of the concept of quality in social care services. A great deal has been written in the last ten years about the importance of quality in human services. Setting standards can make an important contribution to clarity in a service, what's expected of the staff and what users have a right to expect from the service. If standards are set, either by senior managers, by the purchaser or by staff and users, which are unachievable or which are routinely not achieved, the whole exercise becomes a charade.

Defining standards is an important first step, and setting clear, achievable standards contributes to the delivery of a consistent, reliable service which should also meet the needs of users. Four broad approaches to establishing standards are outlined below and comment made on the way in which they should inform best practice.

INTRODUCING STANDARDS

'STANDARD' IS a fascinating word, originally used to describe a flag or military symbol on a pole around which people rallied. The core of this meaning - an agreed focal point around which other people or things can be arranged - has been preserved in the word's later meanings.

Standards are essentially social conventions; we agree on a fixed reference point around which we can arrange, classify and describe any particular example. So, at the most basic level, Napoleon decided that a metre would be a useful unit of length. The choice of this particular length is arbitrary; a decimal system based on the yard or even the cubit might have been just as convenient. Originally intended to be one ten-millionth of the distance between the pole and the equator, the metre was then defined by two marks on a bar in Paris; and more recently by the wavelength of krypton-86. The metre, in turn, provides the reference point for the metric system as a whole. The key thing is to have a standard; one agreed focal point, around which other things can be arranged.

Physical standards, once agreed (the yard was defined in relation to the metre by Act of Parliament in 1963) are fairly dull and uncontroversial. If the village fair runs a 'guess the weight of the cake' competition, losers may argue afterwards about the accuracy of the scales or the ethics of using iron filings. But they are unlikely to regard it as inappropriate to use scales to measure the weight rather than ask an 'expert' to feel the cake; or as simply a matter of opinion as to what the cake weighs at a certain point in time.

At the other extreme, 'artistic standards' are notoriously controversial. Some argue forcefully that it is wrong to use popularity or commercial success as a measure of artistic excellence, while others argue the opposite, and many people would suggest that artistic merit is purely a matter of opinion.

These two issues - defining a standard as a basis for judging a particular example, and the process of making that judgement - lie at the heart of the complexity of using standards in social care. Broadly speaking, the more care is seen as simply a physical process, the more physical standards and unambiguous measurement process can be used. The more care is seen to be an art, the more argument there is about what sorts of standards can be defined, and about how those standards can be applied in practice.

As the word 'standards' is used so widely, common usages have developed which confuse the definition: a person may have high standards; a restaurant may be substandard; a school's standards may have dropped. These usages are different in important ways. The person's 'high standards' are high in relation to our own; and we may mean that they set a high benchmark when judging other peoples' performance, or that they themselves perform at a high level. While these two may go together, it is quite possible for someone to have high standards and be consistently disappointed by their own performance. A substandard restaurant may be meeting the standards it has set itself, while falling well below our own. On the other hand, it is unlikely that the school's Board of Governors has set out some new, low standards to which it now adheres; it is more likely that its performance has dropped.

STANDARDS IN SOCIAL CARE

Standards have proliferated in recent years, so clearly serve some important functions. Three primary functions can be identified.

- To ensure compatibility and comparability
- To assure customers that the product or service is adequate for their needs
- To enhance individual and organisational performance

Compatibility and comparability

Compatibility between different products, systems and technologies is a major issue for manufacturers and distributors who operate increasingly in a global market. Adopting a common 'industry standard' may ensure compatibility at lower cost than 'bolting on' adaptations to conform to the requirements of different markets. Telecommunications and broadcasting are obvious examples where standards are needed to ensure that equipment from different countries can link up successfully. The battles between VHS and Beta-Max video systems, and between Sky and BSB satellite television systems, showed systems that could achieve higher coverage taking precedence over more advanced but less available systems;

because universal compatibility was more important then technical excellence.

Standards have proliferated in every other area of industry, from permitted levels of food additives to the qualifications expected of a social worker. Compatibility between community care services is not technically critical in the way it might be between satellite broadcasting systems (even if users do feel as if their signals are getting bounced halfway round the world before reaching their destination!). Nevertheless, users moving between services may be subject to different models of assessment and different approaches to providing care and treatment; and this may be confusing or even counterproductive.

On the other hand diversity, as long as it is clearly signposted, may be a source of choice and power for the user. For example, the emergence of alternative therapies and ways of understanding health offers people not only more chances of successful treatment but also an important sense of control.

The 'harmonisation' of standards in the European Community serves a number of purposes, depending on a person's point of view: a 'level playing-field' and reduced barriers for international companies; a social democratic endeavour to level-out the quality of life for consumers; a way of excluding imports from outside the community without resorting to tariffs or quotas. Similarly, introducing universal standards in social care in the interests of compatibility (for example, that all staff must have National Vocational Qualifications) may restrict access by consumers to providers who do not fit the mould.

The notion of a single assessment form or a single approach to service provision appeals more to bureaucrats than advocates.

While *compatibility* may be less important for social care than for manufactured goods, *comparability* is increasingly an issue as the purchaser/provider split develops. To use another comparison from the health service: while chiropractic may not be compatible with conventional treatments, it can be compared in terms of outcomes - and it was just such a comparative trail that persuaded the NHS to make this treatment eligible for public funding.

The local authority, in its role as purchaser and strategic planner of community care, needs to compare one service or groups of services with another. To do this, it needs to define standards. What sorts of standards the purchaser decides on will strongly influence the sorts of service that are provided, and the way those services are marketed and packaged.

Meeting customer needs

For customers, standards provide reassurance that a product or service is adequate; and may offer a basis for deciding between different products or services. Customers have access to a huge range of goods, manufactured and assembled all over the world. Symbols such as the British Standards kitemark tell the customer that a product is 'good enough' - and if it turns out not to be good enough there is a right of redress. Similarly, guides like those by Egon Ronay for restaurants, the AA (Automobile Association) star system for hotels or the grading system for carpets are all designed to help the consumer balance excellence and cost. For users of community care services there are, as yet, no such generally accepted signs of excellence, although there are potential pressures from users, purchasers and providers to develop them.

Whether community care *users* develop formal power through individualised budgets from the Independent Living Fund or from the local authority; or informal power through an individual planning or care management system, they will continue to become more assertive and to have higher expectations. Knowing that a service meets certain standards will be an important factor in deciding to use it - particularly for services which have a major impact on the customer's quality of life. The service's standards represent a 'collective contract' with users; what users have a right to expect. By comparison, the 'trial visit' model not only forces the person to move house for a considerable period, but also tends to put the user on trial as much as the service.

The purchaser/provider split will encourage some form of

accreditation, by the *purchaser,* of those providers considered 'good enough' to get public subsidy for providing services. The report on the first 96 appeals to the Registered Homes Tribunal (Harman and Harman, 1988) showed how far we are at present from such a consistent approach. Such accreditation might be in-house; organised by a consortium of purchasers; or based on an external system such as BS5750 (see Chapter 2). This accreditation is likely to be more wide-ranging then current registration and inspection procedures; as providers offer more flexible services, less tied to buildings, there will be a tendency to accredit their competence and quality as providers. The purchaser/provider split may also encourage *providers* to organise some form of independent rating system, as a way both to raise standards and to market services directly to consumers.

Individual and organisational performance

The adoption of a standard, however derived, provides a focal point for a team or organisation to rally round. In this way having standards is important for organisational performance. The consequences of this organisational performance may not please everyone, adopting standards in social care may make an organisation more effective at doing something disapproved of by users, by other professionals or by the local community.

Having standards improves organisational performance in different ways. First, standards spell out what is required; such as every bedroom has a telephone, staff knock before entering rooms. Standards provide a guide to day-to-day work. As a consequence, having standards allows for less direct supervision. Staff know what should happen, so can be given more space to find their own way to make it happen. Norfolk Social Services offer a well-documented account of this process (Cassam, 1990).

Standards can also provide a framework for improvement; the gap between the standard and the practice provides the agenda for change. Equally, if current standards are being met routinely, those standards can be 'ratcheted up' to provide a new challenge.

Belonging to an organisation that has high standards increases staff morale; conversely, once people feel that the organisations's standards have declined, they may find it hard to motivate themselves. Recent writers on management stress the importance of visible leadership and commitment to standards from the top of the organisation.

It is also important to recognise that people who are involved in setting standards should learn about standard-setting; and that people who use standards to compare what *actually* happens to what *should* happen learn about evaluation. These are high-level skills that 'generalise' to most settings; having more people with these skills enhances the organisation's ability to learn.

None of this is without cost, of course. The process of adopting standards in a social care service will cause some disruption and inconvenience however it is done, and the more participatively it is done, the greater the disruption.

Comparisons with industrial standards

Defining and using standards in social care is a more difficult and more complicated process than defining and using standards for, say, carpet manufacturing. This does not mean that it is not worth doing; it does mean that industrial analogies should not be used indiscriminately.

The 'product' of social care

What are those involved with the delivery of social care actually making? Firstly, there is no consensus about the 'product' of social care services. This is not just a disagreement at the margins, like a disagreement between managers in a carpet factory about whether or not to move up-market, or to convert entirely to synthetics. Present-day social care services have evolved from services specifically designed to segregate people and to provide the minimum acceptable levels of maintenance; and while the language, beliefs and intentions of social care practitioners may have evolved, the service models and frameworks have changed much more slowly and erratically. So while a local authority might announce that its social care services are to be judged by the 'Five Accomplishments', its residential care homes may be designed and organised in a way that makes it impossible to deliver the goods.

There is not only a mismatch between form and proposed function; there is also a wider disagreement about fundamental values. A 'prescriptive' view of services sees professionals as the arbiters of need; and the core problems being about ensuring 'accurate' assessments and equitable rationing of resources in relation to those assessments. A 'free market' view of services sees users as the arbiters of need; and the core problems being an equitable distribution of disability income and the development of a diversity of services for people to buy. A 'social change' view of services sees the interaction between users and society as the key issue; and the core problems as helping generic services and structures to become inclusive and helping existing services to keep people in society rather than keep them out. (This lack of clarity is not unique to social care - similar arguments can be made of the education system).

These contrasting views suggest different types of 'product' for social care services and therefore different types of standard. At the extreme, the prescriptive view would seek 'objective' evidence of individual functional performance; the 'free market' view would concentrate on user satisfaction, and the social change view would look at the degree of inclusion and participation by users in society.

Secondly, even if consensus is reached in a particular context about the 'product', it may be hard to develop an agreed model of the production process. In a carpet factory the physical processes are well-understood and easy to separate, both conceptually and in terms of which machine does what. There are consistent linkages between the raw material inputs and the final products, so that a defect in the product can be traced back to a particular input. In many social care services there are no such commonly-agreed linkages, even if there are rules of thumb.

Part of this relates to the impact of the wider environment. A carpet factory is a controlled environment, where production processes are isolated (as far as engineers can manage) from the weather, politics, the people next door, families, individual preferences, and relationships. Social care services are only one factor in shaping peoples' lives; and are primarily about relationships between people, so cannot afford to isolate the process of caring from the particular individuals involved. For example, if 'users manage their own lives' is the 'product' of a support service for people with physical disabilities, a series of standards can be identified for different domains of peoples' lives. But such a service could not be described as a linear process where 'people managing their own lives less' went in at one end and 'people managing their own lives more' came out at the other end. Instead, each individual would, over time, have different experiences, some service-mediated and some not, on which they would bring their own motivation, resources and past experience to bear; and each individual will inevitably change in a unique way.

This is not to say that treating people as incapable is not more likely to encourage incapability; but simply to emphasise that a poor outcome from a social care service cannot be mechanically traced back to a small number of discrete causes. This then creates a tension between defining standards for outcomes (which are not entirely within the service's control), outputs (which are more controllable but may not be good proxies for outcomes), and inputs which are still easier to define and control but may have an uncertain relationship to outcomes.

Finally, the desired outcomes for a social care service may not be seen simply as quality of life for individual service users; but as changes in the wider society (an example might be employers more competent and willing to employ people with disabilities). Introducing social policy issues into standard-setting in social care is analogous to introducing environmental issues into standard-setting in manufacturing; both have far-reaching implications for what counts as quality. The carpet factory's product may be judged purely on whether its output meets the standards specified for quantity and quality, on how well the carpets sell, and on the environmental impact of every stage of the production process. Similarly, a social care service may be judged on its compliance with the terms of its contract with the local authority, on long-term outcomes achieved, or on the impact of every stage of its operation on the wider social environment.

THE PROCESS OF ESTABLISHING STANDARDS

Different stakeholders in the system have a legitimate role in setting standards; and the process has to recognise their respective interests. Stakeholders include providers, purchasers and users. Carers, representative organisations, members of the local community, and professionals with an investment in the service might also be seen as relevant in particular contexts.

For *purchasers*, defined standards for the quality of social care services provide a public framework for making comparisons. Creating this public framework may help the purchaser to direct resources more rationally, although this depends on the sorts of standards that are adopted, and how those standards are used.

Firstly, the standards have to be general enough to allow different types of service to be compared. The Social Services Inspectorate (DoH & SSI, 1990) defines three domains for setting standards for residential care homes: quality of life; quality of care; and quality of management. In relation to many of these issues, standards could be developed that would allow direct comparison between a residential home and an independent living support service.

Secondly, the standards have to be the real criteria for making decisions. There is no point setting out standards for involving users or avoiding institutional practices and then basing decisions on which providers to accredit simply on cost, or the fact that the local authority already does a lot of business with them.

Thirdly, the standards have to be achievable and seen as relevant by the providers - neither an exercise in rhetoric nor an irrelevant set of hoops through which the service has to jump before getting on with the real work.

Standards give *users* some help to make informed choices between services; and greater rights within services. For some users who are dissatisfied it is feasible to change to a different service with higher standards; but, at present, for many people the choice is between their current service and nothing. Knowing that a work support service *guarantees* assistance in getting a person to work on time in the morning may encourage a person with physical disability to undertake employment rather than staying on at a day centre. The knowledge that the day centre states in its users' charter that dissatisfied users have access to an independent arbiter gives the user real leverage.

Providers need to know what purchasers are looking for, in broad terms, so they can direct their efforts accordingly. They also often have their own views about how services should be and about what users want. This is an important consideration; while some providers are providers first and committed to service users second, many social care agencies started from, and still retain, a strong value base. Providers generally do not want all the standards to be set by the purchaser. They want some freedom of manoeuvre; jjust some broad principles to work within, or a process whereby standards are negotiated and renegotiated jointly.

Clearly, however, there is no point in providers setting standards that have unacceptable cost implications for the purchasers on whom they depend.

Within provider agencies, managers and staff of a particular service will also want to 'customise' their own set of standards. Human services are not like fast food outlets as customers want individuality rather than predictability, and staff roles cannot be reduced to a formula and a slogan. The encouragement of local ownership and development of standards within a clear framework of agreed values and methods, is likely to be more effective than the imposition of a rigid system from above.

Similarly, if purchasers or providers set detailed standards unilaterally, users are effectively excluded. While users might not object to the purchaser's standards they will have their own views on priorities, for example preferring support to get out to extra bedroom space in a residential home.

Involving users in setting standards requires that before starting the process consideration is given to:

- establishing the constraints under which the service operates;
- identifying stakeholders and setting up a system for involving them fully;
- clarifying the purpose and product of the services for which standards are to be set; and
- deciding at what level standards are to be set.

The *constraints* on the standards which can be set include regulations on planning, building design, health and safety; equal opportunities legislation and local policy; any local strategic plan for community care; and the purchaser's cost limits. At the level of a particular unit within an organisation's values, policy and practice may also be a constraint.

Clarifying the *purpose* and *product* of the service may be a straightforward matter. Some services and types of service have clear policies and objectives. In other services, it may be simply a matter of bringing together what people already know. On the other hand, many services are in transition from a broadly custodial model towards a broadly supportive and enabling model. In such a service it may be very difficult to agree on what counts as success.

There is no simple formula for resolving this difficulty, whether at the level of a particular unit or a local authority strategy. The usual approach is not to identify this as an issue at all, or to cover it in a form of words that is acceptable to all concerned. The consequence is that useful standards are hard to define; and that staff and users get a mixed message about what is expected of them.

At what level should standards be set?

The setting of standards does not ensure that they are observed in practice. People involved in a standard-setting process have to be clear how the standards they set relate to current practice.

'Ideal' standards can be set by purchasers and providers. However this may result in an 'idealised' view of services and provide a distraction rather than a rallying-point.

Achieving 'ideal' standards depends on many things outside the service's control, hence it is easy to overlook those things which could be done.

'Exemplary' standards are more useful, in that they are the standards of the best current service - the 'exemplar'. People will tend to say 'if we had their resources, or worked in that area, or had their management, we could do as well'; and they are often right. Knowing what is achievable encourages ambitious thinking, but if exemplary standards are intended to guide practice, providers and purchasers have to be prepared to see radical change.

'Normative' standards may be set by the purchaser, or by head office within a provider organisation. The message here is 'this is what we expect to see - if you are performing below these standards, we expect you to do something about it'.

'Ratchet' standards are more likely to be set for a particular service, by the people directly involved. These are defined by looking at current performance and 'ratcheting up' the standards from that performance.

'Minimum' standards may be set by the purchaser for all services to be purchased, in other words, no-one will receive funding to run a service which fails to meet these minimum standards. The provider agency might set minimum standards for all services run by the agency. Minimum standards that are not enforced are clearly not minimum standards, and therefore give a mixed message. For example, if a local authority publishes minimum standards for residential homes for older people yet continues to allow its own homes not to meet these standards, the whole process is discredited. It would be better for the local authority to adopt lower minimum standards and be consistent in refusing to run or fund anything falling below that real threshold.

Once these preconditions have been taken into account, there are four broad approaches to setting standards. These could be called the eclectic, the logical, the 'theme and variations' and the experiential approach.

The eclectic approach

This is the easiest approach to use. Begin by gathering together any policy documents that might be relevant from your own or anyone else's organisation. Look particularly for charters, ten-point plans, codes of practice, matrices. Bring together a group of stakeholders and leaf through other peoples' material. Pull out any bits which sound useful, amend as required, and circulate for consultation.

Advantage The advantage of this approach is that it saves time and effort. For residential services in particular there are already a range of documents available which can be used as a starting-point. Any version you end up with is likely to fall within the broad consensus, and therefore likely to be politically acceptable

Disadvantages These include the following.

- Using the eclectic approach may result in a mixture of standards, some relating to inputs, some to outputs and some to outcomes; some will be ideal, some incremental. Without a clear input-outcome model and an agreed view of the service's current performance, this mixture may prove a poor guide to action.
- The people involved will have avoided thinking too deeply about what the service is trying to achieve or about how they might measure success. They will have invested less in the process and will have less understanding of and commitment to the standards they have set.
- For some types of service, suitable starting points and source material are more difficult to find. For example, standards documents for day services or for area team social work services are not readily available since the desired outcomes for those services are so unclear.

The logical approach

This involves constructing a hierarchy of desired outcomes or accomplishments for the service. This approach was clearly set out by Gilbert (1976). Once a hierarchy of accomplishments has been agreed, standards can be set either for outcomes or for inputs/outputs which make the outcomes more likely. The hierarchy of accomplishments makes it possible to see the relationship between standards. For example, if 'people with disability have a good image' is seen as a high-level objective, then standards relating to publicity and language are of similar importance.

Advantage The advantage of this approach is that it does require some hard thinking about purpose and product. People who have worked through the hierarchy of desired outcomes to establish the standards required will understand their importance and are more likely to be committed to them.

Disadvantage The disadvantage of this approach is that it is easy to do it badly. Common problems include confusing outcomes with plans for achieving outcomes, and lack of practice in breaking down high-level outcomes into components.

There is also a danger of becoming highly prescriptive. Users, staff, carers and managers may start with very different interpretations of the desired outcomes of the service; a consensus version has to be worked at rather than imposed. It may be difficult to frame outcomes and standards which describe the achievements of the service without prescribing for how users should lead their lives. For example, if one of the outcomes agreed is 'people who use the service are not labelled negatively by the service', a standard might be proposed that 'no groups of more than two users and two staff to use local facilities'. If three users share an interest in classical music and they all need personal assistance, is one prohibited from going to a local recital?

In practice, standards may have to be less rigid. For example 'shared activities should reflect shared interests and friendships rather than the availability of staff or transport'; 'users have the right to dissociate themselves from or associate themselves with other service users; staff do not have the right to force association'.

The 'theme and variations' approach

This involves a provider or purchaser introducing a common set of standards for a range of similar services and customising this for a particular service where necessary. This is obviously useful when a provider is running a number of projects with a similar ethos. Projects can be compared in relation to their performance based on the same core standards.

Advantage The advantage of this approach is that it strikes a balance between starting from scratch every time and trying to be prescriptive across a wide range of services and situations.

Disadvantage The disadvantage is that if the standards are defined badly, or are seen by those working in the service as unachievable or irrelevant, this error is compounded across a number of services. The 'owners' of the standards may have spent a great deal of time 'perfecting' them, and be reluctant to alter them just because of criticism from the people meant to implement them. Hence it is easy to reach a stalemate.

In addition, the standards may fail to challenge and even lead to a stamp of approval to inappropriate models of service. For example, developing off-the-shelf standards for Adult Training Centres may distract attention from a radical rethink of their role.

Also, as with the eclectic approach, front-line workers and users may not fully engage with the process; local customising must be seen as an essential part of the process, not an option.

The experiential approach

This approach involves starting from where things are at, looking at current practice and using this as a basis for deriving standards. For example, staff and users might keep diaries for a week, staff and/or users might use a videorecorder or camera to record unobtrusively a day's events; a meeting could brainstorm 'good things and bad things' about the service. This material is then used by a group to agree some achievable standards to be adopted by the service. For example, 'waiting for help to use the toilet' might emerge as a common concern of users; and a standard agreed that 'no-one should have to wait for more than ten minutes', or 'nine times out of ten, people should get help within five minutes of asking'.

Advantage This approach addresses the day-to-day issues in the service, and is based on the things that are seen to matter to users.

Disadvantage Issues which have a bearing on the day-to-day quality of the service are not addressed, either because they are not seen as problematic, or because they are seen as unavoidable, or simply because nobody thinks to mention them. For example, in a supported accommodation project, the main 'dissatisfiers' may quickly emerge as lack of kitchen space and not enough to do at the weekend. Issues such as security of tenure, staff role in relation to tenants, or overall design and decor of the building may get lost. This does not invalidate this approach, but implies that it should be supplemented by other less immediate approaches.

In summary, an eclectic approach may have some value as a starting point for discussion but borrowed standards are a poor substitute for home-grown ones. An 'accomplishments-led' approach will generate a coherent set of standards if done well but in a time of transition will involve some difficult thinking and discussion. A 'theme and variations' approach prevents comparable services from duplicating work and aids comparisons between services but may not be as readily owned, nor help staff and users learn the skills of standard-setting. An experiential approach is the easiest way to promote participation and ownership by staff and users, but unless the facilitator is skilled in ensuring that the group covers the whole ground may result in a partial set of standards.

USING STANDARDS

Setting standards is of little value unless they inform practice. Although this is obvious, it is not uncommon to see a split between the two processes, so that one group of staff in a training section or a quality assurance department is engaged in drawing up impressive sets of standards while the line management system continues to support custom and practice.

For standards to inform day-to-day practice, they should be memorable. 'Everyone who moves into a residential unit is offered a review meeting with their care manager at least once a month for the first six months' is a memorable, programmable and checkable standard. 'All residents should have every opportunity to discuss their stay with the relevant staff at whatever time and in whatever way seems most appropriate to them' may be trying to address the same issue in a more flexible way, but it can easily lead to vagueness about whether the standard has been met.

Standards are a collective contract between the service and users; they do not preclude doing more for a particular individual.

Clearly, the more the monitoring of performance in relation to standards can be undertaken by front-line staff and first-line managers, the more those standards will be owned and understood and the more quickly remedial action is likely to be taken. Nevertheless, periodic formal checks need to be built into the system, both to ensure that standards are being met and to see how far existing standards are still relevant. The standards themselves are not immutable. Once the direction has been set for a service, the broad criteria for good practice are unlikely to change in the short term; but there will be changes in the emphasis on particular aspects and the level of performance expected of the service on the existing criteria. Reviewing standards is essential if the process is to be kept alive.

Figure 4.1 shows the three elements of the quality cycle; defining quality, assessing practice, making changes. Setting standards is about defining quality; unless the other two elements of the cycle are in place, standards are less about quality assurance than about quality reassurance. Unless the standards themselves are reviewed over time, the quality cycle becomes an ever-decreasing circle - and may become increasingly irrelevant to the changing aspirations of users.

Fig. 4.1 The quality cycle

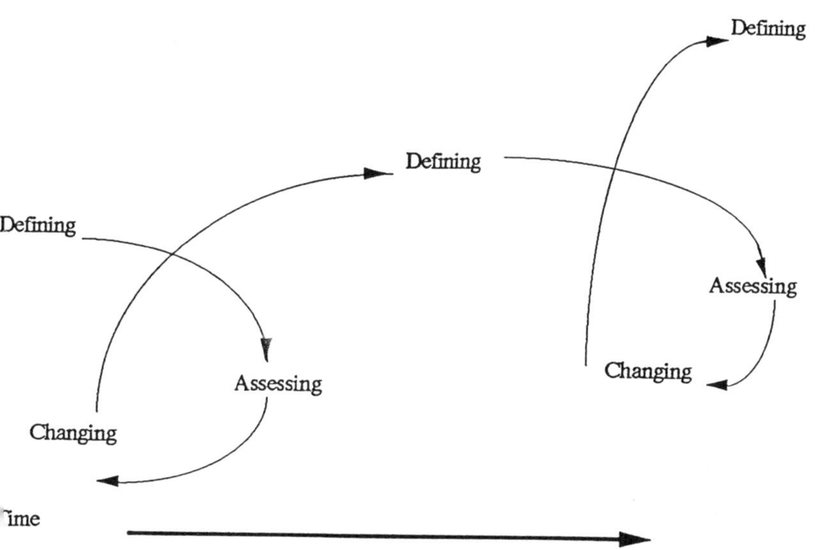

REFERENCES

Cassam, E. (1990). Everything to gain. *Social Work Today,* 19 July.

Department of Health & Social Services Inspectorate (1990). *Guidance on Standards for Residential Homes for People with a Physical Disability.* HMSO: London.

Gilbert, T.F. (1976). *Human Competence: Engineering Worthy Performance*. McGraw Hill.

Harman, H. and Harman, S. (1988). *No Place Like Home.* NALGO.

O'Brien, J. and Lyle, C. (1987). *Framework for Accomplishments.* Responsive Services Associates.

5

The role of inspection and evaluation in social care

Heather Wing

This chapter considers the role of inspection and evaluation in the context of the pursuit of quality in social care provision. It explores the necessary principles and preconditions which underpin an effective inspection process. The author describes inspection and the methods and techniques which are used. One of the primary challenges as Inspection Units begin to function is that of the balance between audit responsibilities and the need to provide development and support, both of these issues are addressed. In addition the use of sanctions is discussed.

INSPECTION AND evaluation are quite clearly methods of quality control. The policy guidance on *Caring for People: Community Care in the Next Decade and Beyond* issued by the Department of Health & Department of Social Security (1989) is unequivocal on this point:

> ...free standing inspection units should be set up within local authorities as a means of checking and promoting the quality of social services in residential and other settings.
> This guidance concerns quality control and focuses in particular, although not exclusively, on inspection of residential care.

Inspection is the process of gathering objective information which can then be measured against stated and agreed standards and requirements. Evaluation is the result of this process pulling together and summarising the overall performance and a determination of the service's value in terms of meeting service user's needs.

Until recently the word inspection has been considered taboo within the personal social services. Instead of 'inspection' several other words have been used, for example monitoring, evaluation, review, quality control, audit, appraisal. In the author's experience, even some of the most senior staff have felt extremely uncomfortable about using the term 'inspection', both in discussion and in the written word. Why should this be? Is it because once you have allowed inspections to be legitimised within one's way of working you have openly acknowledged that there may be shortcomings in the service that you are offering? Or is it that something will have to be done about changing the way one operates, perhaps with considerable financial consequence? There is also considerable fear that those subjected to inspection will experience it as a negative event that could leave the recipient feeling defensive and discriminated against in a way which inhibits development.

The dictionary definition of inspection offers some clues as to why this view prevails:

> To view narrowly and critically, to examine officially... careful survey, official examination... to look into
>
> *Chambers Everyday Dictionary* (1975)

The terms used in this definition carry punitive connotations: small wonder therefore that people regard the process as rather arid with negative overtones and have preconceived ideas about the role of inspection, which in turn shapes their attitudes. I have no doubt that there will be many home owners and managers in all sectors with tales to tell of their experiences at the hands of the 'inspector' in the regulation of the Registered Homes Act 1984, and which mirror the above description.

There may be justification for negative feelings about inspection and inspectors, as some inspectors do take a narrow and blinkered approach to the process of inspections. This is often because, in the absence of clear direction from senior managers within their own departments and, until recently, a lack of interest, many inspectors have simply been left to get on with their own thing. It is much safer to hide behind rules and regulations which are tangible than to broaden the issues and explore the much more intangible issues such as care practice.

The point of this seeming indictment of the inspection process is that the individual carrying out the process is absolutely crucial to the success or failure of the whole operation, and they must have the support of those on whose behalf they are charged with carrying out the task.

Inspection is not just about the process of regulation. It is, through a complex process of relationship building techniques and interaction with a whole range of individuals, a golden opportunity to achieve positive change in the way systems and values are operating, and through this to develop high quality services. Inspection is at the sharp end of stimulating change through quality control. It is a process which is complex, demands a high level of personal skill, knowledge and experience on the part of the Inspector and the sound backing of all those charged with the development of social care policy. If all these are in place the process of inspection can be a rewarding and fulfilling enterprise for all involved.

PRINCIPLES AND PRECONDITIONS

It is essential that the process of inspection and evaluation has a solid value base. The Social Services Inspectorate has done much good work in this respect and guidelines for inspection standards outlined in *Inspecting for Quality* (DoH, 1991) is a significant milestone along the path of social care policy. It states clearly that there are certain principles and preconditions that must exist for the Inspection Units, set up by the Social Services Department in April 1991, to effectively undertake their quality control functions in an evenhanded and independent way. The key principles are given below.

The inspection process should be:

- *rooted in explicit values and measurable standards,* which should be publicly available;
- *publicly accountable at all levels* by a variety of means, eg. reports, press articles, public meetings;
- *devoid of discrimination* in all respects relating to service users and staff;
- *impartial* in respect of all agencies, all people who receive service and all methods of measurement, and this impartiality should be *demonstrable*, so that service users and carers will have confidence in the inspection process. The process should be *equitable* in applying the same rules in similar circumstances;
- *visible* in its activities and information should be widely available;
- *consistent* in it's method of operation;
- *reliable and without prejudice* and based on objective evidence which could be independently validated;
- *flexible* and allow for unforeseen circumstances; and
- should help give *protection to users*, be regular, and sometimes unannounced.

The guidance document suggests that, in order for these principles to be adhered to, it is essential for certain preconditions to exist. The list given below includes further preconditions which the author feels are significant. The preconditions are listed in order of priority as seen by the author.

1. Explicit legislative base and authority to proceed.
2. An agency value in, and commitment to, the inspection task, evidenced by adequate provision of staff with appropriate remuneration in recognition for the degree of skills required, other resources and clear support systems.
3. Clear statement of values, aims and objectives at agency and unit level that all concerned subscribe to and are committed to achieve.
4. Existence of staff, or commitment to recruiting staff, who have the necessary skill, knowledge, experience and belief in the inspection process and the maintenance and promotion of high standards of service.

5. A statement as to who will carry out inspections, how, when and where, including a clear distinction between the different roles the inspectors may be asked to undertake.
6. Clear procedures defining how inspections will be carried out.
7. Guidance on what is to be examined and the standards against which judgement will be made.
8. Clear methods and techniques to conduct evaluations.
9. Arrangements for ensuring deficiencies and problems are put right and for checking on remedial action progress.
10. System for reporting - to whom results should be reported.
11. A reliable support network at agency level including a supervision process to ensure that officers receive direct monitoring of their needs and performance.
12. Clear procedures for decision making on major policy and resource issues arising from inspection reports.
13. Clearly specified role and relationship between the function of inspection and that of other quality mechanisms within the agency.
14. Arrangements in place to evaluate/audit the inspection/ quality control mechanism periodically to ensure that it continues to maintain credibility and integrity of purpose.

AIMS AND OBJECTIVES FOR INSPECTION

The aims and objectives for inspection should reflect accurately the value base of the agency and be expressed in simple phraseology that can be easily understood. The main *aim* of inspection is to provide a process, outside of line management, which is rigorous, systematic and strictly objective in evaluating standards and which is regarded an enabling and positive in it's intentions to promote good quality standards.

In this respect the main *objectives* to achieve the above stated aim could be as given below.

- Ensure that statutory requirements are being met and that policies, where they exist, are being implemented.
- Ensure that users' quality of life does not fall below standards that are accepted as 'good enough'.
- Contribute to the promotion of higher preferred standards wherever possible.
- Involvement of users and staff at all levels in the inspection process.
- Encourage service providers to assume appropriate levels of responsibility towards service users.
- Ensure that processes such as staff recruitment, management, support and training are effective.
- Identify poor practice and suggest remedial options and, in the event of no change, be forthright in the use of sanctions whenever these are clearly indicated.
- Disseminate good practice for the benefit of all.
- Informing those in charge of policy and decision making of issues requiring wider consideration.
- Be prepared for scrutiny of own effectiveness in ensuring the quality of service provided.

THE INSPECTION PROCESS

The inspection process is more than just ticking boxes, using a tape measure, or proceeding through a checklist in a detached and impersonal way. It is a complex interaction of individuals on a certain day in a certain place at a certain time. It requires the inspector to utilise knowledge, skill and experience of a variety of issues along with the use of their personality and ability to engage the service provider in something that is seen, by both, as meaningful. Only if this latter aspect is successfully undertaken will there be any real progress as a result of the inspection.

Sir William Utting, Chief Inspector, Social Services Inspectorate stated in an address, in January 1990, to Directors of Social Services and elected members:

> Inspection should not be taken to mean aiming simply at the elimination of unacceptable standards, but should include the positive promotion of better

standards through a developing process of partnership with homes (managers, staff and residents) in all sectors.

In the same address Utting drew attention to the fact that regulatory inspection is principally concerned with the 'observance of regulations and standards, made in order to protect or provide additional security, for people who depend on others for their care...' Inspection is a safety net or insurance against the institutional and institutionalised abuse of very vulnerable people. It is not in itself a means of promoting the pursuit of quality services, for which it must add the capacity for commenting authoritatively on policy, organisation, professional practice and the use of resources.

It is clear that inspection can serve both to *assess* and *promote* quality of social care provision, although it is essentially a tool, the effectiveness of which is determined by the use to which it is put. Inspection can and should be a *positive* process in the service of managing for quality.

However before an inspection can take place there must be in existence a broad base of consensus between inspectors and inspected about values and practice. Whatever guidance is produced must assume that the credibility of any inspection rests ultimately on the professional abilities of the inspectors. 'There is no place for a merely *routine* approach to inspections'.

The following suggests the various stages all inspectors should move through as they undertake each inspection.

1. All inspections should be *planned and prepared* for, even if they are to be unannounced. This will involve appraising oneself of the service's characteristics, the client group served, the functions, the size and the sector.
2. Inspectors must *identify specific issues* they wish to concentrate on, stemming from pervious inspections, complaints received or general issues in existence.
3. They must equip themselves with all necessary *'tools' to measure performance,* i.e. guidance documents, legislation, reference material.
4. If the inspection is to be announced the *time of inspection must be communicated* well in advance to allow for

mutual preparation.

5. Sufficient *time to conduct inspection*, and cope with unforeseen circumstances, should be scheduled.
6. The *appointment* (if announced) *must be kept.*
7. The manager/owner of the service must be clearly informed of the *nature and purpose of the inspection* and the time should be structured accordingly.
8. The inspection must be conducted in a *professional, courteous and impartial manner.*
9. Respect for service users *privacy and rights* should be a priority throughout the inspection.
10. There should, wherever possible, be space to provide *regular feedback* to owner/managers during the course of the inspection and to enable an *exchange of views.*
11. Observations, discussions and *evidence of findings* must be *recorded* throughout.
12. All judgements should be based on *objective measurements against* agreed standards and requirements. However, where an inspector feels it necessary to include an 'intuitive' comment there should be scope to do this.
13. *All aspects of care should be explored* in as unobtrusive manner as possible.
14. At the end of the inspection a *summary feedback* should be provided to the owner/manager in private. Shortcoming should be clearly stated and suggestions given as to how these can be rectified, plus deadlines where necessary. Good practice should also be identified.
15. The service provider should be left with a *sense of value* and not demoralised by the experience.
16. The inspection must be followed up promptly with a *detailed typed report*, outlining service shortcomings, identified good practice, recommendations and requirements for change, suggestions to resolve certain issues and deadlines for change to be undertaken.
17. The service provider must be given time to *respond* to the contents of the report. Further discussion may be necessary to confirm the inspections findings.
18. Inspectors must *check periodically* on service providers *progress* on actioning recommendations and requirements.

The following flow chart summarises the process for announced inspections of all residential care homes in Surrey. (The structure of the day will vary from home to home depending on the service, e.g. in a service for people with learning difficulties who are out all day at a Day Centre an inspector may have to come back in the evening to meet with residents.)

FLOW CHART

1. Date of inspection fixed in advance.
   Letter sent stating date, time, name of Officer.
   Notice to be displayed prominently within home also enclosed - informing residents, staff, visitors of inspection date and time, and inviting contact with inspector if required.

2. Officer reads reports, identifies issues for scrutiny.

3. Collects all relevant 'tools' for inspection.

4. Arrives on time at service to be inspected.

5. Brief introduction to the day and the purpose of the inspection, domestic arrangements agreed. Identifies aims and objectives of the service, are these explicit and owned by staff, are they appropriate to client group cared for?

6. Tours building to assess physical environment in terms of clients' needs and stated aims and objectives. This evaluation of the physical environment also serves to announce the inspectors presence within the home to staff, visitors and the residents. Notes issues for discussion, good practice aspects and shortcomings. Draws these to managers attention at the time wherever possible.

7. During evaluation of physical standards uses opportunity to talk to residents and staff.

8. Discusses outcome with manager/owner.

9. Scrutinises records/administration, discusses with manager/owner reasons for certain practice, or lack of it. Suggests remedies for change where necessary. Identifies good practice and links needed for efficient administration with all round care of individuals such as care plan records, control of medication, staff records and knowledge of all necessary procedures.

10. Takes meal with residents wherever possible, and if they do not object (this should be paid for by the Inspector). Observes quality of food, presentation, staff attitude to residents, interaction of residents, special needs. Discusses life in the home with residents.

11. Provides brief feedback to manager/owner about observations on mealtime.

12. Discussion with owner/manager about care practice, needs of residents, staff abilities to care, their training needs, staffing levels in terms of client needs and dependencies.

13. Discussion about health care, links with primary health care team and other professionals, needs of residents.

14. Discussion with manager/owner about social care, recreation, links with the community.

15. Discussion with residents and staff where possible.

16. At conclusion of inspection gives summary feedback, shortcomings measured against stated standards and requirements. Suggests options to explore to achieve change and deadlines for compliance with requirements. Identify good practice.

17. Give space to owner/manager to also give feedback on experience of inspection and plans for action.

18. Follow up inspection within two weeks with detailed typed report, clearly stating findings and evidence for these, the appropriate action to be taken where explicit and suggestions for change where recommended good practice. All required action must have stated reasonable and realistic deadlines. Good practice must be clearly stated.

19. Report offers owner/manager further opportunity to comment and where necessary to meet with Inspector if factual inaccuracies or findings where evidence may be suspect. A deadline is given for the owner/managers response to the report and if none received it is assumed that the owner/manager will abide by the requirements.

20. Further checks made later to identify progress on action points.

In Surrey it was decided that the statutory second 'unannounced' inspection (required under the Registered Homes Act 1984) would be used as an opportunity to obtain purely consumer feedback. This inspection can take place at any time and is designed to ensure that the maximum number of residents can participate in the process. As a lead-in the Inspector checks on the progress of previous recommendations made and then selects certain themes as a focus, for exampleprivacy, choice and risk taking, for discussion with residents. An aide memoire is used by inspectors to facilitate the interaction with residents. Discussion takes place either in small group settings or individually. During the process there is also space for some discussion with staff away from residents and, if present, for relatives and other visitors. At the end of the consumer feedback session the Inspector gives feedback in detail if the owner/manager is available. If not, staff members are advised that a report of the findings will follow. A consumer feedback report is then provided to the owner/manager on a prescribed format and time is allowed for their response to the recommendations and requirements contained in this report. Again, if no response is received within a prescribed period, then it is assumed that the owner/manager agrees to the contents. To avoid the tedium of ploughing through endless repetitive paperwork the Inspection Unit has introduced a pre-inspection questionnaire which is used periodically for the announced inspections.

The cycle of inspections encompassing all the various contacts used in obtaining formal information is set out in Figure 5.1 overleaf.

Placing the inspection in context

Figure 5.1 describes the administrative and scheduling process rather than the content and purpose of inspection.

In considering the 'why' of inspection it is useful to turn to the distinction drawn in the Social Services Inspectorate documents (DoH, 1990; 1991) between quality of care and quality of life. Taking into account the wide range of issues that make up quality of care and quality of life, Figure 5.2 may be a useful depiction of the total focus of inspection.

The main focus, which is evident from Figure 5.2 , is the service user, and the way in which care inputs are experienced as outcomes by users. This complex interaction of processes is constantly changing and there will always be a need to take stock periodically by asking, 'How are we doing?'. In the first instance this will be the prime task of

Fig. 5.1 The cycle of inspections for new registration.

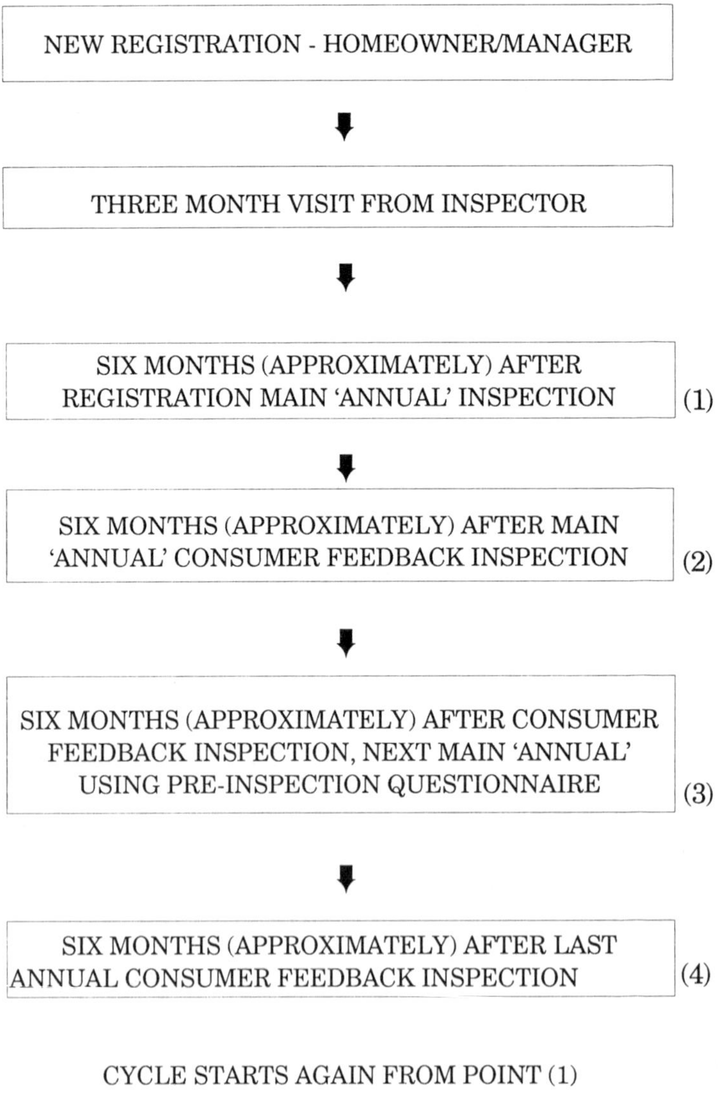

NEW REGISTRATION - HOMEOWNER/MANAGER

↓

THREE MONTH VISIT FROM INSPECTOR

↓

SIX MONTHS (APPROXIMATELY) AFTER REGISTRATION MAIN 'ANNUAL' INSPECTION (1)

↓

SIX MONTHS (APPROXIMATELY) AFTER MAIN 'ANNUAL' CONSUMER FEEDBACK INSPECTION (2)

↓

SIX MONTHS (APPROXIMATELY) AFTER CONSUMER FEEDBACK INSPECTION, NEXT MAIN 'ANNUAL' USING PRE-INSPECTION QUESTIONNAIRE (3)

↓

SIX MONTHS (APPROXIMATELY) AFTER LAST ANNUAL CONSUMER FEEDBACK INSPECTION (4)

CYCLE STARTS AGAIN FROM POINT (1)

the manager and staff. The inspection serves to ensure that this process of reflection and 'stocktaking' produces a positive experience for service users.

In order to thoroughly evaluate all these aspects it is clear that it is not possible, nor indeed acceptable, to spend the whole period of the inspection within the confines of the manager's office. This denies valuable opportunities to use evaluative techniques and it devalues the inspection. It is not fair to the service provider and their staff as it will not be possible to obtain a rounded picture of the service delivered.

To do justice to how a service truly operates it is desirable, in the first instance, to spend at least one full day enquiring, listening, hearing, observing and discussing as many aspects of the service users care as possible in a structured way. There is much to be gained in sitting down with a group of staff and/or residents, generating discussion on what it is like to work within the service or what it is like to receive the service. Listening to responses, observing interaction: the extent of participation and the content of responses can tell you more about how the service operates than many other forms of performance measurement.

It has often been suggested that 'it is no use asking service users for their views particularly in residential care because they will be frightened to bite the hand that feeds them'. Although there will always be individuals that choose not to talk to an outsider about the care they receive, either because of fear or of feeling disloyal to the service provider, it is usually possible to find users who are happy to discuss the service they receive and propose useful suggestions for service improvement. However it takes considerable skill to engage a group of service users or an individual in such a discussion, time needs to be given to establish a degree of trust and some reassurance given that information supplied will be treated in a discreet and professional manner.

It is important that inspections are never confined to a '9-5' weekday period. The business of caring for people, particularly in residential care, goes on 24 hours a day, 7 days a week, 365 days a year. It is therefore essential for the credibility of the process to inspect services early morning,

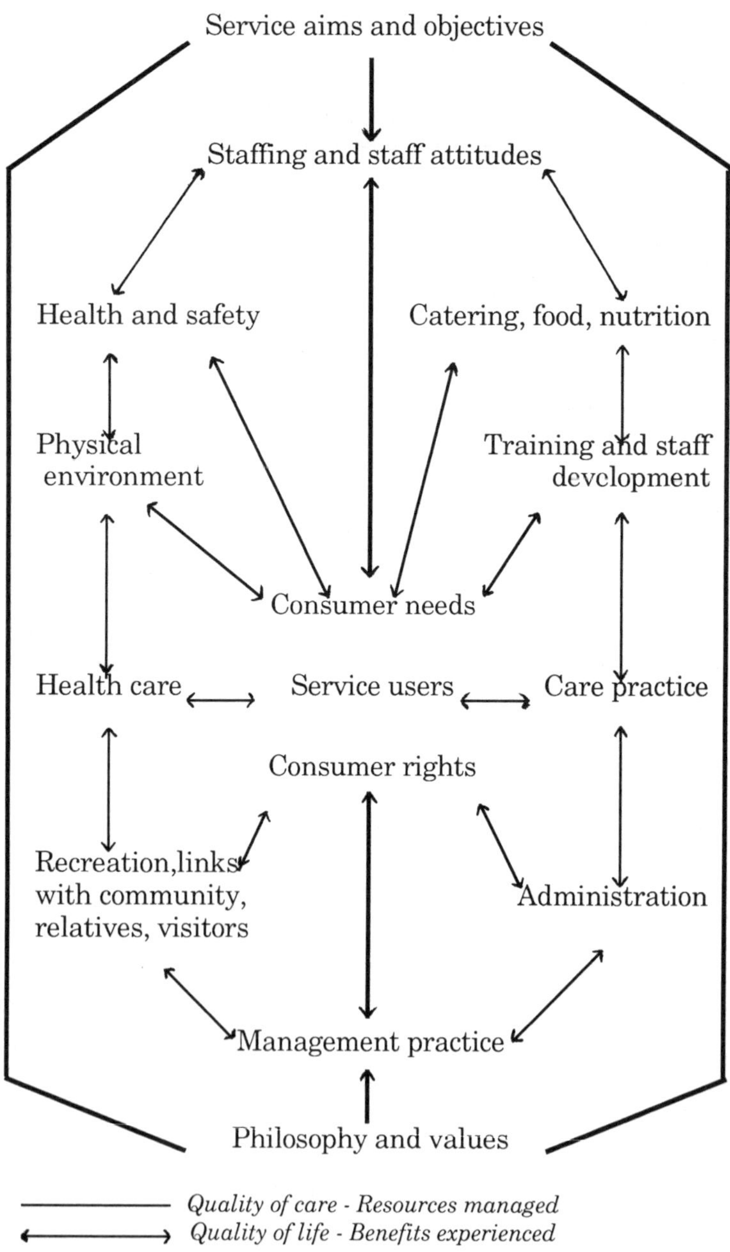

Fig. 5.2 The total focus of inspection

late evening, at weekends and at times such as Bank Holidays. The Inspector may not be popular when arriving on Christmas Day, but service providers will be in no doubt that the business of inspection is being taken very seriously indeed.

Inspection - methods and techniques

Given that there is no established training programme on how to carry out inspections, the following is offered as some of the techniques and methods of evaluation that officers have used.

- *Direct observation* e.g. staff interaction with service users, condition/presence of facilities.
- *Direct questioning* e.g. asking service users and staff for comment on certain issues.
- *Direct testing, sampling and checking* e.g. using call system in a bedroom to test if working and staff response time, sampling a meal, asking staff what the procedure is in the event of a fire.
- *Discussion* and exchange of views formally and informally with service *providers.*
- Use of *questionnaires* to invite comment from service users.
- *Inviting written or telephone contact* from service users and service providers.
- *Informal discussion* with service **users** and their families.
- *Visiting unannounced* at different times, day and night during a week.

In all respects the inspection should be viewed and conducted as an enabling experience for all concerned. It should be seen as an opportunity to learn, to develop, to put on show good practice and innovation and for the building of positive relationships between the inspector and service provider in the furtherance of good quality service standards.

There will always be a natural reluctance and resistance to scrutiny and an unwillingness to accept criticism and advice, however constructive. However inspectors are the lynch-pin in the inspection process and their resoluteness in the face of such feelings is vital. It follows, therefore, that it is a task which should be undertaken by staff of the highest calibre in personal and professional terms. In addition, it is essential that a comprehensive national training and development programme for inspection staff is established.

The inspector must be pragmatic and flexible in terms of policy guidance and avoid creating unnecessary barriers to appropriate care and development. An ability to negotiate, and if necessary compromise, with dignity in the interests of the service user is a requirement from both the inspector and service providers point of view.

The following suggested time allocation for a typical inspection provides for an effective use of resources.

- Half a day preparation, paperwork, planning meeting.
- One day to conduct inspection (this is an average, some services may take more time, some less).
- One day to write up report, discuss with senior if there are difficulties, despatch report, liaise with other services and deal with recipients queries.
- Half a day to undertake follow up on report's recommendations particularly if deadlines for compliance are very short.

On average, each inspection takes three full person days. To undertake the two statutory inspections per year per establishment required under the Registered Homes Act 1984, six person days will be required per establishment per year. Based on an average available days per year per inspector of 230 (deleting weekends and holidays), in theory each inspector can only take on approximately 38 establishments per year. This figure takes no account of the investigation of complaints, appeal and tribunal work, and time required to be spent on other duties such as registration, dealing with general public enquiries about standards, attending meetings, supervision and training sessions and general management of workload. It follows therefore that, if 'quality' inspections are expected, inspectors must be freed from the pressures of high workloads in order to devote the necessary time required for the task. Taking these factors into account there is a need for formal guidance on acceptable ratios of services to be inspected by individual inspectors.

LINKS WITH SUPPORT AND DEVELOPMENT

Whilst accepting the key objectives of ensuring adherence to statutory requirements and evaluating standards of service offered, inspections can also provide managers and policy makers with valuable information about a specific aspect of service. For example, if all inspections over a certain period of time focused on a particular theme such as catering, staffing levels or training, this information would provide ample evidence for decision making in respect of specific action to be taken. Indeed the inspection task should be seen as wider than simply periodically carrying out checks on services.

It is a valuable opportunity to offer advice and support to service providers and users. It is clear, as has been reinforced in the Social Services Inspectorate report *Inspecting for Quality* (DoH, 1991) that inspectors should never take over the management role. The report notes that it is important to be clear about what is meant by 'development' and 'advice and support'. They suggest and endorse that inspectors will 'as a matter of course provide feedback to homes, both formally and informally on the outcomes of inspections and this will include suggestions and recommendations for improving services'. This is seen as an advisory and supportive role. On the other hand the report states categorically that 'enabling those improvements to take place is clearly a developmental role and is primarily the business of line management'.

Most inspectors will have direct experience of working in the caring professions. Their knowledge, skill and experience will be wasted if it is not shared in terms of offering advice and support to service providers during the course of inspections and indeed after these have taken place.

Although service providers/managers are expected to

identified shortcomings and developing the service, not to provide them with advice at the point of identification seems to be unrealistic and unreasonable. It is important to be aware that many service providers, particularly within the private sector, have few immediate support networks to draw on. There is no place in the inspection process for ideological and political stances over the role of private sector care - all service providers have the right to the same degree of advice and support.

One of the most important things to evaluate is the preparedness of managers to listen to advice and their willingness to take this on board and institute improvements in standards. The key to this process of offering advice and support is that the inspector, when placed in this position, should retain his or her capacity to make dispassionate and objective evaluations of services. The SSI make a further point on this issue (DoH, 1991).

> This does not rule out the development of constructive relationships between inspectors and the staff of the homes inspected - indeed it emphasises the need for them. But where conflict may arise between the inspector role and the advisory and supportive role the inspector role must come first...

For experienced officers this may not be a problem, however for new and inexperienced officers there is a clear need for specific guidance in this respect.

QUALITY AUDITS

A quality audit fulfils a number of purposes.

- It is a means of ensuring greater accountability between an enterprise and the community at large.
- It is an independent means of checking that the systems in place to exercise quality control are working and are effective in promoting good standards.
- It is a means of periodically checking certain standards to provide crucial management information to influence decision making.

In many ways the enhanced role of the Social Services Inspectorate in monitoring the work of the Inspection Units set up in April 1991 is a quality audit role. *Inspecting for Quality* states that, 'the annual reports of local units and the individual reports they produce on service will provide the SSI with a basis to monitor the effectiveness of the Units' (DoH, 1991). There is a clear mandate to monitor not only the operational framework of the Inspection Units but also 'it's role and functions' within the Social Service Departments, and also the full range and outcomes of this role and function. The Advisory Committee, if established with explicit terms of reference and a commitment to the task, will also have the potential to act in a quality audit role.

This quality audit function can be achieved in a number of ways.

- Regular visits by Advisory Committee members to services to check on how the quality control system is working.
- Committee meetings.
- Ensuring that service users comments and ideas on service received are listened to and taken seriously.

In the process of auditing, 'auditors' will constantly need to be aware that quality is a standard, a goal or a set of requirements. Quality is a measurable goal, not 'a vague sense of goodness'. It is a continual effort to improve, rather than a set degree of excellence. Quality is an elusive goal, a moving target, once attained it must be maintained and sustained and improved upon as complacency is unacceptable. Quality audits make a statement to the public that those responsible for quality assurance are taking the business of quality control seriously. Periodic systematic and independent checks to ensure that services are actually achieving what they set out to achieve keeps everyone 'on their toes' and provides the spark for continued improvement to practice.

Quality auditing can provide valuable information for the improvement and development of services. The audit could focus on specific aspects of service delivery, for example, catering, staffing levels and their impact on consumers. Concentrating in depth on a specific subject provides a wealth of information on which to base future policy and practice decisions. The survey conducted by Counsel and Care, *Not Such Private Places,* demonstrates how much attention can be given to a specific area of care and the impact that such an 'audit' can make on the thinking of policy makers and service providers (Counsel and Care for Elderly Persons and their Carers, 1991). In addition there is a crucial place for quality auditing within the arena of quality assurance, in a sense to 'check on the checkers'.

USING SANCTIONS

The use of sanctions can take two main forms: the formal processes that can be used to ensure adherence to standards such as recourse to law; and the informal processes that can operate, which can directly affect quality standards.

Formal sanctions

Sanctions in the formal sense, through recourse to law, are an essential part of quality control. They can be used from the outset to ensure compliance with certain standards as evidenced in applications for registration under the Registered Homes Act 1984. If a person fails to meet the required standards then their application for registration is refused. Required standards are usually met because of the incentive to be registered.

Although this course of action is traumatic for the applicant the service user is not yet part of this scenario and therefore the effects of sanctions are limited to an individual. Once a service is established sanctions, or the implied threat of their use, remain a crucial tool in the quality control process.

It is acknowledged that there is an inextricable link between quality control and sanctions, implicit in the word 'control'. Yet scarcely a mention of it is made in quality assurance literature and it is not mentioned at all within *Inspecting for Quality* (DoH, 1991).

Some Local Authorities have been accused, by service providers within the independent sector, of being too 'Gung Ho' in the use of sanctions, preferring to use this means of achieving change rather than using powers of persuasion, negotiation and compromise. Others have been accused by lawyers, journalists, politicians and researchers of being too fearful of using sanctions in case they upset service providers and because of the likely cost of litigation. The ideal lies between the two where a commitment to the achievement of high service standards is agreed.

It is, however, not easy for an inspector to seek recourse to law to achieve required standards. One of the many concerns is the lack of willingness on the part of their Authorities to support them when sanctions are clearly indicated. There are many examples which can be cited of a reluctance or inability to proceed because the local authority:

(i) were not prepared to cover the cost involved;
(ii) did not want to upset the independent sector where they were a major provider of care;
(iii) had political pressure placed upon them; or
(iv) were fearful of losing face and of receiving bad publicity if they lost the litigation.

This has greatly undermined the credibility and confidence of inspectors and has incensed those within the independent sector who are also committed to high standards of care. Nonetheless, before formal sanctions are used there should be clear evidence in place of efforts that have been made on the part of the inspector to promote an improvement in standards. This will include inspection reports, follow up letters and reports, records of telephone contacts, additional visits, correspondence from other parties and the recorded outcomes of all these interventions. The required improvement to standards of care should be explicit, reasonable and realistic to attain and appropriate to the service users concerned. If there is clear evidence that every effort has been expended to achieve the required standards and the situation continues to be unacceptable, then officers have a duty legally, morally and professionally to proceed in the use of sanctions. The responsibility then passes to management at all levels and, in the case of Local Authorities, the Social Services Committee. They are accountable to the public and have a duty to care for vulnerable people. If they shirk this responsibility by refusing to authorise sanctions where clearly indicated then their reasons for doing so must be made publicly explicit.

It will be interesting to see what type of sanctions can be brought into play when public sector services are exposed to the same level of scrutiny as those within the independent sector. This is likely to be a highly charged and emotional issue for many people, as no legislative powers have been granted to impose the same requirements as those for the independent sector. Inspection and Registration Officers are prepared for the task of inspecting public sector services to the same standards as those within the independent sector. However there is much justifiable disquiet as to what inspectors can do if local authorities refuse to comply with requirements on standards. Surely this is one of the craziest situations ever created by policy makers, when the employers of the quality control officers refuse to comply with their own statements on quality standards.

I remain optimistic that this situation will resolve itself in time, and predict that formal sanctions (such as closure) will be imposed on authorities by their own committees, as poor standards are made more publicly explicit. This will be achieved in a number of ways.

- Publicly available inspection reports
- Advisory Committees who will receive reports on standards in all sectors
- Establishment of structured and publicly explicitly complaints procedure
- Service purchasers requiring better value for money

Informal sanctions

There are a number of other ways that sanctions can be used in the process of quality control. These include the following.

- Peer group pressure from other service providers, Homes Associations
- Professional body pressure, e.g. Social Care Association (SCA), United Kingdom Central Council for Nursing, Health Visiting and Midwifery (UKCC), Royal College of Nursing (RCN), British Association of Social Workers (BASW)
- Professional 'users' of the service such as General Practitioners, Social Workers
- Local and national media
- Service users and their families
- Market forces

It is surprising how much the above can contribute indirectly to the process of quality control. Peer group pressure can be extremely difficult to resist if you desire to be part of that group and you are debarred because your standards are out of tune with others. Those who hold well-earned professional qualifications may well fear the possibility of professional disqualification if they fail to adhere to the organisations aims and values. There cannot be many of us who would not be alarmed at the prospect of bad publicity at the hands of the media, and in the case of the service provider the effect this may have on the service. Perhaps inevitably the biggest influence on the service is likely to be that of the fear of the service not being utilised and therefore going out of business.

With soaring interest rates, higher wage bills and other expenses, competition for service users will be increasingly fierce. Although this may well mean that some small services disappear because they are no longer viable it also means that the writing is on the wall for those services who continue to offer poor service. There is increasing emphasis on the empowerment of service users and notice taken of their views. Inevitably therefore those services that offer the best value for money will survive, those who do not will cease to exist.

CONCLUSION

At present we are awash with a plethora of guidance documents and new policy statements about quality assurance and the role of inspection within this process. The terms 'Quality Inputs', 'Quality Outcomes', 'Quality Assurance', 'Total Quality Management' and so on imply that there is a clear understanding of what is to be achieved to attain a good quality service. The reality is that it is inordinately difficult to define what is meant by quality, and to define a satisfactory level of quality that is acceptable to all concerned.

Quality is viewed differently by everyone: the professional, the manager, and the recipient of the service. However all three have important contributions to make and whilst it may be impossible to have a totally objective definition of quality care, we can strive to agree sets of mutually acceptable standards of quality.

Quality implies 'all round excellence', therefore a systematic programme which incorporates the consumer perspective is vital. Such a programme requires the full commitment and leadership of senior managers. Ultimately the final level of output quality measurement is service users views and opinions about the service they receive. This area has, until recently, been consistently neglected by those responsible for quality assurance. With the arrival of the 'new breed' Inspection Units, inspection and evaluation of personal social services has risen from it's 'any other business' position on the agenda to one of the top priorities for consideration. Their place within the quality assurance arena is key. They have the opportunity to develop consumer empowerment by positively encouraging consumer participation in the quality control process. There is now no place for sloppy, ill thought out, amateurish approaches to quality control. The time has now arrived for a systematic, structured quality control process to find it's rightful place in the furtherance of quality services for all consumers.

REFERENCES

Chambers Everyday Dictionary (1975). W & R Chambers Ltd.

Counsel and Care for Elderly Persons and their Carers (1991). *Not Such Private Places: Survey of Private Homes in the London Area* (February).

Department of Health (1988). *Towards a Climate of Confidence*, Report of a National Inspection of Management Arrangements for Public Sector Residential Care for Elderly People. London: HMSO.

Department of Health & Department of Social Security (1989). *Caring for People: Community Care in the Next Decade and Beyond*. Cmnd 849. London: HMSO.

Department of Health (1990). *Regulating Residential Care*, Report of Bournemouth Conference. January 1990. (unpublished).

Department of Health (1991). *Inspecting for Quality: Guidance on Practice for Inspection Units in Social Services Departments and Other Agencies. Principles, Issues and Recommendations*. London: HMSO.

South West Thames Regional Health Authority (1988). *Quality: The Strategic Approach*. Policy Proposals (June).

6

Checklists: their possible contribution to inspection and quality assurance in elderly people's homes

Ian Gibbs and Ian Sinclair

This chapter introduces the notion of checklists as a means of monitoring quality in social care services. It draws on a research project commissioned by the Social Services Inspectorate in anticipation of the work of the Inspection Units set up by Social Services Departments in April 1991 as part of the community care legislation. The authors outline the features of the research project which illuminate aspects of this inspection method and contribute to the debate about how quality can be assured in social care settings such as residential units for older people.

UNDER PROPOSALS set out in the White Paper *Caring for People* (DoH & DSS, 1989), and given substance by the National Health Service and Community Care Act 1990 local authorities were required, from April 1991, to establish 'arm's length' inspection units. The new units, independent of the day to day line management within social services departments, are charged with inspecting and reporting on both local authority and registerable independent residential care homes and, most crucially, applying the same quality assurance criteria to all homes. In pursuit of this objective the Department of Health (1991) has issued guidance to registration and inspection staff on the conditions to be expected in a good home. Of particular interest is the stress placed by the guidance on the need to take into account the quality of care provided and the quality of life for residents as well as the physical conditions.

While quality assurance has received much attention in the National Health Service, especially since the implementation of reforms proposed by Sir Roy Griffiths in 1983, local authorities have not until recently been under the same pressure to develop quality assurance programmes. This is not to say that quality issues in residential care have been considered unimportant - indeed much time and effort has been directed at the task of inspecting and regulating homes. Even so, inspections continue to give the major emphasis to the compliance of homes with various safety regulations and other relevant legislation. The varied and numerous existing forms and schedules used by local authority inspection staff reflect a clear emphasis on the relatively stable or 'structural' features of the home - for example, the width of corridors, space per resident, the number of bathrooms provided or the cleanliness of the facilities. By contrast very little attention has been given to the quality of care and quality of life for residents, who are likely to live in the home for a number of years, and for whom some of the home's most important features are those denoted by 'comfort', 'respect', 'homeliness' and other equally intangible concepts. While a handful of existing forms attempt to measure quality issues in a systematic way, few, if any, have been subject to rigorous tests for validity and reliability.

The importance of quality of care, and the need to include relevant measures for its assessment, are highlighted in the Wagner Report (National Institute of Social Work, 1988). The committee received numerous requests calling for improvements to the system of inspection and registration, and in particular for quality of care to be regarded as more important than quality of buildings. Evidence submitted to the committee provides further support for the view that quality of care should be an essential component of the inspection process. One of the organisations submitting evidence noted:

> A monitoring system that concentrates on physical facilities rather than on the sensitive issues of care has made it possible for bad practice to exist in homes that have passed all the registration requirements.
> (National Institute for Social Work, 1988, p.202.)

So much is perhaps readily agreed. The practicalities of assuring quality are harder to achieve and three issues in particular arise.

- Is there an agreed philosophy of care which would allow measurement of its quality?
- If so, can inspectors judge care reliably in the sense that one inspector is likely to agree with another on the quality of care in a home so that their judgements are not arbitrary or idiosyncratic?
- Is it possible to identify the determinants of quality (e.g. staffing ratios) so that steps can be taken to remedy low quality as they can be taken to implement fire regulations?

These are the issues which will be considered in this chapter.

In tackling these questions the authors draw on material from a research project commissioned by the Social Services Inspectorate (SSI) within the Department of Health. Relevant parts of the study are described at different points in the chapter, but in general it was commissioned by the SSI as part of the preparation for the new independent inspection units. The study involved the department of social policy and social work at the University of York and five local authorities (two boroughs and three counties) in different regions of England. Each authority selected an agreed number of homes from the local authority, private and voluntary sectors yielding a total sample of 48 homes - 16 local authority, 24 private and eight voluntary.

The overall aim of the project was to assess the validity and usefulness of a checklist approach for the new arm's length inspection units and to contribute towards the debate over inspection methods. It should be emphasised that the use of a checklist is only one among a range of approaches to the inspection process, and that the validity which might be established for checklists is not necessarily generalisable to other methods of inspection nor to the inspection process as a whole.

A PHILOSOPHY FOR DEFINING AND MEASURING CARE

The approach to defining quality which had most influence on the present project was the one developed by Donabedian (1980) for assessing quality in health care and in other long stay settings. He labels the three major approaches to quality assessment in terms of their focus on *structure*, *process* and *outcome*.

Structure represents the relatively stable characteristics of the providers of care, the resources they have at their disposal, and the physical and organisational settings in which they work. Many of the checklists currently used by local authorities concentrate on structure, and Donabedian offers two highly relevant comments on this approach: first, that it is an indirect and rather limited route to assessing quality of care; and, secondly, that the relative stability of many aspects of structure means that regular monitoring is probably unnecessary.

The *process* of care is the set of activities which take place within and between those who provide care and those who receive it. There are two major influences on the process of care: first, a set of 'technical' norms which, in the case of health care, are largely determined by the state of medical science and technology at any given time. Secondly, there is another set of norms which are derived from the principles that govern the relationship among people, in general, and those providing care and those receiving it, in particular.

Whereas process is the most direct route to an assessment of the quality of care, *outcome*, similar to structure, provides a less direct approach. In this context, an outcome denotes those aspects of a resident's well-being which can be linked directly to the care provided. As such, it includes the social and psychological functioning as well as the physical condition of the resident. A major limitation of the outcome approach is the difficulty of determining whether changes in a resident's functioning and well-being are due to the care provided or to other causal factors outside the influence of the home.

Donabedian offers structure, process and outcome as a guide rather than a straitjacket. Nevertheless, the rationale for his three-fold approach is that a 'fundamental functional relationship exists among the three elements'. For example, the structural characteristics of the settings in which care takes place influence, either positively or negatively, the process of care. Likewise, changes in the process of care, including variations in its quality, will influence the effect that care has on the physical and psychological well-being of residents.

The analysis offered by Donabedian, combined with the evidence presented in Wagner (National Institute for Social Work, 1988), was seen as sufficient justification of a need to concentrate in this project on process rather than on structure or outcome. Nevertheless, Donabedian's idea that structure, process and outcome were linked encouraged the authors to measure some variables which could be considered structural, for example, staffing ratios; and some which might reflect outcome, for example, occupancy ratios, on the grounds that this variable might reflect poor care.

Having decided to give special emphasis to process the next task was to identify sources of items for the checklists to be developed. For this task the authors were able to draw on two major developments concerned with quality of care and quality of life in residential settings.

The first was the work of the group which had prepared *Homes Are For Living In* (DoH & SSI, 1989). The group argued that the many factors which contribute to quality in homes grouped naturally around the following six basic values: Privacy, Dignity, Independence, Choice, Rights and Fulfilment. Statements about the 'good' home become the criteria against which professional judgements can be made about the standards in the home in question. For each of the six basic values in the original document, an aide memoire contains a range of indicators which enable judgements to be made about the extent to which practice matched the criteria.

The second approach to the problem of measuring care, but one which nevertheless differs slightly in emphasis, was developed by Jonathan Bradshaw and colleagues at the University of York. This approach was derived from *Home Life* (Centre for Policy on Ageing, 1984) with the individual items organised around five core principles.

- *Choice and autonomy* Rights, freedom, independence, control, risk-taking, responsibility
- *Individuality* Self-expression, identity, privacy, personal space, individual needs
- *Personal competence* Physical and mental functioning, addressing the needs of the whole person
- *Participation* Meaningful relationships, access to and integration with the local community
- *Value* Respect, dignity, appearance, valued social role, beauty of surroundings

The approaches embodied in the work of the *Homes Are For Living In* group (DoH & SSI, 1989) and Bradshaw can be envisaged as operating at three levels. A large number of evaluative 'items' or indicators concerned, for example, with choice of food are grouped within a smaller number of broad dimensions, concerned, for example, with the provision of choice in general (see Fig. 6.1), and these in turn are linked to an overall evaluation of the home. In this way the approaches provide a link between the detailed observations of inspectors and the final judgements they may need to make.

Fig. 6.1 Basic evaluative structure of the two checklists.

Level 1	Evaluative items or indicators
Level 2	Basic values or core principles
Level 3	Global judgement

It is important to note that the form and content of the checklists outlined above are only two among a range of possibilities.

WAS THE PHILOSOPHY ACCEPTABLE TO INSPECTORS?

Two residential conferences brought together a number of very experienced inspectors from the SSI and the five local authorities. The first conference was devoted to briefing them on their task, and modifying the instruments to be used in the light of their comments; the second allowed them to reflect on their experience of the inspections, and raise a large number of issues relevant to the feasibility and value of attempting to assess residential homes in this way.

The inspectors identified a number of possible purposes in using a checklist. In particular, checklists could form part of a fuller quality control system; provide a method of monitoring the consistency of inspections; provide evidence to tribunals concerned with deregistration; further the development of homes; or yield material for a star rating or 'Michelin system' which, if published, would provide the public and case managers with relevant information when choosing homes.

In achieving these purposes, inspectors felt that the checklist should be consistently applied by different inspectors, yield conclusions which could be defended and easily understood, cover all aspects of a home of interest to inspectors, provide appropriate judgements of quality and be capable of administration within a reasonable time span. In short, the checklist had to be reliable, defensible, intelligible, comprehensive, valid and practical.

Against these criteria the instruments used in the project were seen to have a number of limitations. For example, they were in part repetitive, they took time to complete and gave insufficient coverage to the traditional material of inspection and inadequate attention to racism. These criticisms reflected the deliberate emphasis of the instruments on quality of care and quality of life, and the limitations of any instrument being tested for the first time.

A more serious problem was the difficulty inspectors found in making many of the judgements required. These included concerns about the following.

- *The status of the evidence* How far, for example, reliance could be placed on staff reports as against observation?
- *Multiple criteria* How, for example, should inspectors balance the choice allowed in some respects against the lack of choice allowed in other?
- *Uncertain standards* When should the line be drawn between acceptable and unacceptable practice, particularly given professional uncertainty over, for example, the management of risk?
- *Lack of allowance for the unexpected* For example, the lack of mention of the difficulties which could arise because of a depressed proprietor or one with idiosyncratic views.
- *Imprecision in rating systems* For example, the difficulty of deciding whether to rate '3' or '4', i.e. 'probably yes' or 'definitely yes'.

In addition to their comments on the instruments, the inspectors made a number of suggestions on the procedures and organisation required if the instruments were to be used effectively. Their comments covered the need for training; the occasional use of two inspectors for the same home to promote consistency; greater use of observation and discussion with residents; and efforts to ensure the acceptability of the checklist with the different groups and parties involved.

In spite of their critical comments about the specific shortcomings of the checklists used in the project, those who had carried the inspections still felt that the approach had considerable merit. It was also reported that heads of homes were positive about the potential of this different type of inspection. The difficulties they experienced concerned the methodology rather than the philosophy of care. As will be seen below, this conclusion was in keeping with the statistical data collected.

CAN QUALITY OF CARE BE RELIABLY MEASURED?

The difficulties found by the inspectors in completing the ratings suggested that the ratings themselves might be unreliable in that different inspectors might not rate the same home in the same way. The research design of the project enabled this possibility to be tested.

The fieldwork took place in two stages - Stage 1 involved a visit to each of the 48 homes in the overall study by a member of the inspection staff from the local authority. Half the sample of homes (Group A homes) in each of the five areas was visited by an inspector from the local authority using the checklist derived from *Homes Are For Living* In (the HAFLI checklist) (DoH & SSI, 1989); the other half of the sample (Group B homes) was inspected by a second local authority inspector using the second checklist derived from Bradshaw's work (the York checklist) (see p.107).

At Stage 2, about four to six weeks later, homes were re-visited by a different inspector to the one who had made the first visit. Thus, Group A homes were inspected twice: once at Stage 1 by an inspector from the local authority and again at Stage 2 by either a second inspector from the local authority or by an inspector from the Social Services Inspectorate. On both occasions inspectors completed the HAFLI checklist. Similar arrangements applied to the Group B homes, with the inspectors using the York checklist for both visits.

The fact that the homes were inspected twice allowed cross-tabulation of ratings made on the first and second visits to see whether agreement was significantly greater than chance, and in this way to test their reliability.

In carrying out this analysis data from the checklists was used. The main part of the data provided required assessors to make a professional judgement on 'items' of care based on their experience of inspecting residential care homes and an interpretation of the evidence they had managed to assemble during the six hour visit. In order to test the reliability and scaleability of this part of each checklist, assessors were asked to indicate on a 4 point scale - *Definitely No, Probably No, Probably Yes* and *Definitely Yes* - whether the home was meeting the criterion reflected in each of the evaluative items. Guidelines were offered for making these evaluative judgements.

In addition to the ratings for the evaluative items inspectors were also asked to provide a global rating of the quality of care in the home *'taking into account all the items ... rated in the previous sections and any other important considerations not covered'*. For this purpose they were given a scale with six values ranging from *extremely poor* (1) to *extremely good* (6).

In presenting the results it is easiest to begin with this global rating of quality - the third level of evaluation in Fig. 6.1. Overall, the agreement between the inspectors on this rating common to both checklists was statistically significant (r = .38 and it was higher, although not significantly so, among raters who had used the HAFLI checklist than among those who had used the York checklist (r=.51 as against r=.29). While statistically significant these correlations are far from large; a correlation of r=.51, for example, accounts for only about 25% of the variation.

A possible explanation for the modest correlations could be that inspectors were agreed on the characteristics of the homes but differed in the weighting they gave them in coming to an overall evaluation. For example, they might have agreed that the home scored highly on the warmth and quality of the interactions between staff and residents and low on privacy. If, however, they differed in the importance that they gave to these two dimensions of home life, they would have differed on their overall evaluation of the home.

In practice this explanation is implausible for two reasons. First, it was generally true that inspectors who rated a home high on, say privacy, also tended to rate it high overall. The pattern of results did not suggest that the inspectors disagreed over whether privacy or the other dimensions covered in the checklist were not important constituents of a good home. Second, there was no evidence that inspectors were in better agreement over lower level items than they were over higher level ones.

Table 6.1 presents the results for the 49 evaluative items within the HAFLI checklist; the first level of evaluation in Fig. 6.1. It can be seen that few of the correlation coefficients are in excess of .40, in statistical terms a low threshold.

Table 6.1 Correlation between ratings over two visits for HAFLI items

Value	*Privacy*		*Dignity*		*Independence*	
Item	1	.49	1	.14	1	.25
	2	.37	2	.32	2	.05
	3	.48	3	.19	3	-.06
	4	.28	4	.66	4	.06
	5	.28	5	.25	5	.53
	6	.60	6	.25	6	.47
	7	.40	7	.34	7	.09
	8	.28	8	.04		
			9	.58		
Value	***Choice***		***Rights***		***Fulfilment***	
Item	1	.23	1	.06	1	.18
	2	.36	2	.13	2	.00
	3	.30	3	.04	3	.37
	4	.15	4	.35	4	.12
	5	.50	5	-.03	5	.08
	6	.06	6	.10	6	.48
	7	-.10	7	.14	7	.04
			8	.28	8	.34
			9	-.09	9	.31

Two items drawn from the basic value 'Dignity' provide a practical example of what the correlation coefficients imply. Tables 6.2 and 6.3 cross-tabulate the judgements from the two inspection visits for one item where there was a large measure of agreement between the two inspectors and another item where the opposite was the case.

Table 6.2 Cross-tabulation of judgement for two visits–Item E2.4 from the HAFLI checklist (Pearson Correlation = 0.66)

(The home has knowledge and takes account of residents' past life and present situation when caring for them)

	Second Visit			
	1 Definitely No	2 Probably No	3 Probably Yes	4 Definitely Yes
First Visit:-				
1 Definitely No	-	-	-	-
2 Probably No	-	**1**	-	*1*
3 Probably Yes	-	-	**10**	4
4 Definitely Yes	-	-	4	**4**

***Note**: Exact agreement in bold; major 'outlier' in italic.*

Table 6.3 Cross-tabulation of judgement for two visits - Item E2.8 from the HAFLI checklist (Pearson Correlation = 0.04)

(Residents know what information is kept about them)

	Second Visit			
	1 Definitely No	2 Probably No	3 Probably Yes	4 Definitely Yes
First Visit:-				
1 Definitely No	-	2	*1*	*1*
2 Probably No	*1*	**2**	2	-
3 Probably Yes	1	5	**7**	2
4 Definitely Yes	-	-	-	-

***Note**: Exact agreement in bold; major 'outlier' in italic.*

The greatest disagreement is when inspectors differed by more than one rating category in their judgements. For example, in Table 6.2 there is only one major 'outlier' - the occasion when the inspector for the first visit to one home said *Probably No* and the inspector for the second visit said *Definitely Yes*. Another form of disagreement, but perhaps less serious, is when one inspector says *Probably No* and the other says *Probably Yes* (of which there are no examples in Table 6.2. Table 6.3, on the other hand, contains three major 'outliers' and seven instances of the *Probably*

No:Probably Yes form of disagreement.

For reasons of space the results for the evaluative items from the York checklist are not presented here but, by and large, they follow a very similar pattern to the results for HAFLI. From a practical point of view this apparently low degree of agreement for the individual evaluative items in each of the checklists poses considerable problems. For example, agreement at this level does not provide reliable backing for tribunal decisions. Nor is it adequate to explain the findings on the grounds that the inspectors were undertaking the artificial task of making ratings. Any quality control system based on inspection is likely to require an inspector to assess whether a home is satisfactory in certain respects. If the reliability of such judgements is low, this casts doubt on an apparently essential element of arm's length inspection.

CONDITIONS FOR IMPROVING RELIABILITY

The rather discouraging results given above encouraged the authors to try and identify conditions in which inspectors were able to make more reliable judgements. First, the question *Does the type of inspector make a difference to the reliability?* was posed. By limiting the analysis to those homes where both visits were undertaken by local authority inspectors a large proportion of the correlation coefficients did improve. However, not too much should be read into this result because, taking account of the small number of homes, the relevant statistical tests indicate that the second set of correlation coefficients was not significantly different from the first set.

The next step was to see whether a 'better' measure of quality could be obtained by combining the more reliable items and excluding the less reliable ones. For this analysis the two items with the highest correlation coefficients between the first and second visits were taken from each of the six basic values within HAFLI. These were added together in order to create an overall score based on the 'best' items. Given that only the 'best' items were chosen to create the new total score it is not surprising that a correlation coefficient of 0.63 was yielded by this analysis. However, this is not a great improvement on the coefficient of 0.51 yielded by the Level Three global score from Fig. 6.1. So, even limiting the analysis to the 'best' items failed to remove all instances of major disagreement between inspectors, or to greatly improve on the reliability of the global assessment they made of the home. The results were similar for a scale of 'best' items from the York checklist.

The next question to explore was whether the level of agreement between inspectors visiting the same home was affected by whether they carried out their activities in a similar way. According to their own accounts the time they spent in the home on the first inspection varied from 200 to 600 minutes with the most common and median figures being 300 minutes. Within this period the estimated time spent with the head of home varied from 45 minutes to 420 with the most common and median figures being 180 minutes. In about half the first inspections (46%) the inspectors talked to a group of staff on their own.

In three-quarters of the visits inspectors spoke for five minutes or more with at least three residents on an individual basis and, in addition, during 36 of the 48 visits they also talked to residents in a group. The only routine they almost always recorded observing was the provision of a meal. A wide variety of other activities were observed on occasion but only toileting, the medication round, and recreational activities were observed on over 30% of the first visits.

For this analysis five activities were examined: talking to staff; talking to residents; talking to head of home; contact with family, friends and fellow professionals; and the routines observed. From these five items a summary variable, called 'thoroughness', was created. This reflected the degree to which inspectors reported above average (the median) involvement in their various activities. In relation to each of these variables the visits were divided into two groups: those where the inspectors were highly involved (e.g. spent more time than the median amount of time with the head of home); and those where they were less involved. The hypothesis was that where inspectors had been highly involved in a particular method of gathering evidence on both visits, they would be in greater agreement in their overall evaluation of the home than where they had been less involved or differed in their approach. As can be seen from Table 6.4 there was no evidence for the hypothesis. Indeed the relevant correlations were generally lower if both inspectors had spent an above average amount of time in a particular activity.

Table 6.4 Correlation between global scores on first and second inspection visit in selected groups

		Correlation
1. Talking to staff		
	High talk on both visits	.29
	Other*	.39
2. Talking to residents		
	High talk on both visits	.21
	Other*	.48
3. Talking to head of home		
	High talk on both visits	.13
	Other*	.49
4. Contact with family, friends, professionals		
	High contact on both visits	.33
	Other*	.42
5. Routines observed		
	High observ. on both visits	.14
	Other*	.53
6. 'Thoroughness'		
	Greater on both visits	.25
	Other*	.48

***Note**: Other* = either 'low' on both visits or 'low' on one and 'high' on the other*

The last form of analysis was to examine whether the sector of care - local authority homes or private - made a difference to the reliability. This provided a very striking result. The correlation between the global evaluations made on the first and second visits was -.07 for local authority homes and .58 for private homes. Roughly speaking, in local authority homes there was no agreement between inspectors on how good the home was while in private homes the agreement was well in excess of chance.

THE DETERMINANTS OF QUALITY OF CARE

Given that in the private sector, although not the public, there was some evidence that inspectors agreed on the quality of life in the home, what seemed to determine this quality? In order to investigate this question, measures derived from the first inspection were used and the authors tried to relate them to judgements of quality made at the second. This avoided the possibility that apparent causal relationships arose because the inspector believed them to exist (for example, because an inspector who judged that the staff were enthusiastic was for that very reason more likely to judge that a home was good, thus giving rise to an apparent relationship between 'goodness' and staff enthusiasm).

A number of analyses of this kind were carried out, but only those which were simple and gave rise to significant results are given below. These concerned the following variables all of which were measured at the first inspection visit.

- *Leadership* A rating of the quality of leadership exercised by the head of home.
- *Sufficient staff* A rating of the degree to which the inspector felt that adequate numbers of staff were on duty at key times of the day.
- *Staff qualifications* The proportion of care staff, including the head of home, who had a relevant nursing, social work (CQSW) or CSS qualification.
- *Occupancy* The proportion of registered beds occupied by residents at the first inspection.

In addition, a composite measure consisting of the global rating of quality from the first visit, the rating of the leadership of head of home, and a score based on the proportion of trained staff (1 if home fell in bottom third of homes on this measure, 3 if it fell in the top third and 2 for the middle third) was created. This measure allowed the authors to see whether a score which reflected structural as well as process variables was a better predictor of the global judgement of quality made at the second interview than a simple judgement of quality on its own.

Table 6.5 sets out the correlation between these variables and the overall global rating of quality made at the second interview. The findings suggest that in the private sector the quality of care is related above all to the leadership exercised by the head of home and to the proportion of trained care staff. For reasons discussed in the conclusion these relationships should not necessarily be taken as causal although they are of considerable interest. The relationships between 'sufficient staff' and the global score at the second interview would also have been of interest if only the authors could have been sure that the judgement of quality truly reflected quality rather than the idiosyncratic impression of the inspector.

Table 6.5 Correlation between selected items and global score from second visit for local authority and private sector homes

	Correlation	
Variables correlated	Local Authority	Private
1. Leadership/Global 2	.18	.55
2. Whether sufficient staff/ Global 2	.60	.15
3. Staff qualifications/Global 2	.11	.60
4. Occupancy/Global 2	.14	.34
5. Composite measure: (Global 1+Leadership+ Staff Quals)/Global 2	.11	.75

The correlation between the composite score and the global rating of quality for private homes is the highest the authors have so far reported, accounting for 56% of the variation in the second global judgement. Table 6.6 sets out the relationship for the private homes in tabular form. For the composite measure private homes have been divided into two groups: those with a 'below average' score; and those with an 'above average' score.

Table 6.6 Cross-tabulation of composite measure with the global score from the second visit - private sector homes

	Global 2					
	Extremely poor	Very poor	Poor	Good	Very good	Extremely good
Composite measure:						
Below average	-	-	5	5	2	-
Above average	-	-	1	-	10	1

Though not shown in Table 6.6, of the 'worst' four homes on the composite score from the first visit, three were rated 'poor' at the second visit and one 'good'. Of the 'worst' nine homes, five were rated 'poor', 3 'good' and one 'very good' at the second visit. Similarly, the 'worst' nine homes on the composite measure contained all but one of those subsequently rated 'poor'; however, the 'worst' four homes on the composite measure contained only three of the six homes rated 'poor' on the second visit.

CONCLUSION

The issues raised at the beginning of this chapter concerned the philosophy that might underpin judgements of quality, the degree to which quality could be reliably measured, and the factors that might determine quality of care. What can be learnt about these issues and what are the implications?

The authors' conclusions on the philosophy of care in homes are, as far they go, encouraging. Important work has undoubtedly been accomplished in this area, not least by the Wagner Committee and the groups which produced *Home Life* (Centre for Policy on Ageing, 1984) and *Homes Are For Living In* (DoH & SSI, 1989). The inspectors in the study found checklists based on this work congenial to use and felt that they directed attention to areas which were too easily overlooked in inspection. Their criticisms were related to the methodology they were required to use rather than to its philosophical base. Their judgements on, for example, the amount of privacy afforded by a home were related to their judgements on the overall quality of the home in the way that was consistent with the emphasis on privacy in previous work.

This conclusion, while pleasing, should not give rise to complacency. In the first place there is a need to test the validity of the philosophical base itself. Clearly elderly people are unlikely to disparage the importance of choice or privacy or the other values which underlie *Homes Are For Living In*. What is not known is how important these values are to them in comparison to others. Are most elderly people relatively unconcerned about choice of food (a key issue in most assessments of quality) but very concerned over whether the staff appreciate their jokes or value their idiosyncrasies (not something to which much attention is paid)? Is it possible for homes to subscribe fully to the values of *Home Life* but nevertheless be soulless places in which to live?

A second issue concerns the degree to which these values are widely accepted and are embodied in procedures other than inspections. If staff in homes do not accept these values, they will not accept the validity of inspections based on them. If the regulations governing tribunals do not endorse the possibility of de-registering homes on the grounds of poor quality, inspections concerned with quality lose much of their force. If residents and relatives are not aware that these values are officially endorsed they will be less likely to complain or approach inspectors if the values are not followed. One value in devising a checklist embodying ideas about quality is the message carried that quality is important. The message, however, is likely to be blurred if the philosophy of quality is not widely disseminated and discussed.

A third issue obviously concerns the degree to which quality can be reliably measured. In practice the importance of reliability is likely to vary with the aims of an inspection. If an inspection is concerned with questions of registration or with providing guidelines to the public or case managers on what is a good home, reliability is crucial. The judgements of an inspector are unlikely to be given much weight at a tribunal if a second inspector is as likely as not to come to a different conclusion. Similarly it would seem unfair if a judgement on the quality of a home which was likely to affect its ability to attract residents was essentially based on nothing more than a personal opinion. If on the other hand inspection is concerned with improving performance, reliability is less important. It is an altogether easier task to point to things which need improvement than to come to a reliable judgement on what is an average or above average home.

In these respects the authors' findings suggest that:

(i) it is difficult to make reliable judgements on the quality of aspects of care in homes, and very difficult indeed to make reliable judgements on the quality of care in local authority homes; and

(ii) notwithstanding the above it is possible to pick out 'poor quality' private homes at a first inspection which have a high probability of being judged 'poor' at a second inspection.

These findings have relevance to the kind of methodology employed in inspecting homes and to its aims.

In relation to methodology the authors would argue that a checklist is more likely to be useful as an aide memoire reminding inspectors to cover certain areas and motivating heads of homes to consider these areas than as a mechanical instrument yielding a score on which homes pass or fail. The judgements made are complicated and these need to be reflected in the technology. For similar reasons the main thrust of inspections is likely to be to improve performance rather than to make dubious judgements of quality which are given a spurious impression of accuracy by being expressed in numerical form. In this context inspections will be only one of a variety of instruments (self- assessment, complaints procedures, and training may be others) designed to improve the quality of care.

This said, inspection may still play a role in quality control. It has been seen that, in the private sector, it is possible to identify a small minority of homes - say 10% of those inspected - which are judged to be poor on first inspection and will be similarly picked out on a second inspection. These judgements of quality are probably more reliable if they combine three different kinds of information - the inspector's overall rating of the quality of care, a separate rating on the leadership exercised by the head of home, and information on the proportion of qualified staff in the home. These results suggest that it should be possible to set up a quality control system in which a minority of homes were identified as giving cause for concern, and selected for fuller inspection (involving perhaps interviews with residents) or for 'remedial help'. If a home failed to improve, it would be possible to take it to a tribunal with some confidence that the judgements of quality on which the authority was relying did not simply represent the whim of the inspector.

De-registration is inevitably a last card. It takes time, is an uncertain business, and raises awkward issues over what is to happen to the residents in the home concerned. For these reasons it is important to identify the factors in a home which influence quality and which may supply the leverage necessary to improve it.

In this respect the project's findings on the determinants of quality in private sector homes are important. They suggest that quality depends on staffing, and in particular on the leadership exercised by the head of home and the proportion of trained staff in post. Both findings, or rather the conclusions based upon them, require testing. For example, it could be that 'proportion of trained staff' is simply a proxy for generous provision which is reflected in high standards in other areas - for example, the standard of accommodation and food. It may be this lavishness rather than training which produces high quality. Moreover even if trained staff produce higher standards in the current system, there is no guarantee that they would continue to do so when the new system of training is brought in.

The importance of testing these findings lies in their relevance to improving the quality of homes. The data support the idea that the quality of head of home is crucial to the quality of establishment. In other residential establishments this is almost certainly true (Sinclair, 1975); similarly Kitson (1990) has shown that the ward sister's concept of care is the most influential factor in determining the quality of care of elderly people in hospital. This suggests that it should be possible to devise policies designed to ensure that only people who had demonstrated a capacity to run such homes were allowed to do so (as only certain people are allowed to captain ships). Research could also be targeted at identifying the differences between successful and unsuccessful heads of homes, thus leading to more efficient identification of poor heads and better training for them. Equally if it could be shown that the training of staff does influence quality (again there is relevant research from the field of nursing, Gibbs *et al.*, 1991), it would be possible to raise the general quality of the system by insisting on a given proportion of trained staff in any establishment.

These comments on quality control and the determinants of quality do not apply to public sector homes for the simple reason that the authors were unable to obtain reliable measures of quality in this sector. The reasons for this failure must be a matter for speculation. It was not, as far as the authors were able to assess, that inspectors gave local authority homes an easy ride. Perhaps it reflects the greater complexity of these homes. An inspector who talked to five residents in a small local authority home would have sampled a higher proportion of residents than would be the case in a large local authority one. The heads of home in the private sector are likely to exercise a powerful influence on what goes on, so that the time spent with them may enable the inspector to form a reliable judgement of a key element in the regime. By contrast the influence of the head of home in the local authority sector may be more hedged around with regulation, and constrained by key members of staff or union agreements. Different shifts in local authority homes may differ more than they do in private homes, so that inspectors observing them may effectively be observing different regimes. Whatever the explanation, the absence of any correlation between the judgements of inspectors on the quality of homes in the local authority sector must be a matter of concern and one which suggests an urgent need for further research.

Although the findings given here are inevitably provisional they confirm the complexity of the inspection process. They do not suggest that a simple checklist can allow accurate measurement of quality, or remove the risk that an apparently acceptable home is the setting for inhuman and degrading treatment of residents. At the same time there is a positive element to what has been found. The development of an aide memoire based on *Homes Are For Living In* (DoH & SSI, 1989) is likely to be welcomed by many inspectors and will encourage a recognisably different form of inspection. This inspection should both concentrate attention on key elements in the life of a home and provide a basis for a simple system of quality control.

In conclusion, the full benefits of this study will only be realised when comparative data on alternative inspection methods become available. This in turn requires the setting up of a coherent programme of research on different approaches to quality assurance.

REFERENCES

Centre for Policy on Ageing (1984). *Home Life: A Code of Practice for Residential Care*. London: CPA.

Department of Health (1991). *Inspecting for Quality. Guidance on Practice for Inspection Units in Social Services Departments and Other Agencies: Principles, Issues and Recommendations.* London: HMSO.

Department of Health & Department of Social Security (1989). *Caring for People: Community Care in the Next Decade and Beyond*. Cmnd 849. London: HMSO.

Department of Health &Social Services Inspectorate (1989). *Homes Are For Living In*. London: HMSO.

Donabedian, A. (1980). *The Definition of Quality and Approaches To Its Assessment*. Ann Arbour, Michigan: Health Administration Press.

Gibbs, I., McCaughan, D. and Griffiths, M. (1991). Skill mix in nursing: a selective review of the literature. *Journal of Advanced Nursing, 16*, 242-249.

Goldberg, E. and Connelly, N. (1982). *The Effectiveness of Social Care for the Elderly*, London: Heinemann.

Kitson, A. (1990). *Therapeutic Nursing and the Hospitalised Elderly* . Royal College of Nursing Research Series London: RCN.

National Institute for Social Work (1988). *A Positive Choice.* Report of the Independent Review of Residential Care. Chaired by Gillian Wagner. London: HMSO.

Personal Social Services Council (1975). *Residential Care Reviewed.* London: PSSC.

Sinclair, I. (1975). The influence of wardens and matrons on probation hostels. In Tizard, J., Sinclair, I. and Clarke, R. (eds), *Varieties of Residential Experience.* London: Routledge and Kegan Paul.

7

Training for quality

Roger Clough

This chapter addresses two aspects of training in relation in quality assurance - training for quality and quality in training and argues that they are inextricably linked. Quality in training is enhanced by defining the aims and objectives of each training programme, selecting the appropriate method, involving participants and learning from experience. An audit of training needs on an individual and organisational basis should be undertaken in order to ensure the relevance of training.

'TRAIN, TRAIN, train' states the author of a Department of Trade and Industry (1989) guide to *Leadership and Quality Management.* Indeed, it would be hard to find a self-respecting book on quality assurance which did not emphasise the importance of training. The Wagner Report (National Institute for Social Work, 1988, pp.90-1) suggested that every establishment:

> should be required to draw up a staff training plan which should be subject to inspection procedures. The plan should be closely related to the aims and objectives of the establishment, and to its specific function and tasks.

The recommendation was that such plans include induction training, core training, team development and regular appraisal of training needs.

Further evidence of the importance which may be attached to training is to be found in the fact that organisations are sometimes assessed according to the percentage of their budget which is spent on training. There is a current debate at a national, political level as to the damage which is being done to the economy by a failure to invest in training, a debate which would be of some interest were it not for the fact that it has been repeated so often over the last hundred years.

Yet perhaps one of the reasons why, in spite of the rhetoric, trainers do not always hold high status is because of the doubts many people have as to the value of training. We know that it is necessary but wonder whether it achieves anything at all. This is particularly the case in relation to training for practical tasks: are social workers (or teachers) born or made? Can you teach people how to counsel others, to talk or listen? Is it appropriate to train home care staff?

I am both a fierce defender of the importance of training, to the extent that I dislike people using the word 'academic' in the sense of having no relationship to the real world, and yet a critic of much of what goes on under the banner of training. I have seen individuals and groups of staff influenced by their experiences so that they work more effectively. Yet, I have also seen some slapdash work. It must not be forgotten that much training is very expensive in terms of the fees of the trainers and the lost work of the staff. Do we know if it is worth it?

There is also the issue of the way in which a balance may be maintained between a recognition that there are skills in training and an avoidance of the pretension which, inappropriately, turns the whole task into a mystique. It may help to define 'training'. Here, the word will be used in the sense of a conscious attempt on the part of one person or people to instruct others in the tasks and skills which are pertinent to performance at work.

The process of training may have beneficial side effects, for example in that time away from work, sometimes in pleasant surroundings, may provide an opportunity to recharge. Sometimes the attachment of the word 'training' to activities has been used to lend respectability, which in turn has been used to justify expenditure. The issue is not that 'time away' may not be of immense value and is an entirely proper activity on which an organisation may wish to spend money. The point is that it would be healthier if there were straightforward definitions of task and expectation, so that if 'time away' is wanted, it does not have to be hung on the peg of training. Too often that sort of device has led to grandiose claims being made in the name of training, which are not realised and result in training always being justified by grander assumptions than the activity warrants. On the other hand, busy people may resent attendance at a course which is badly structured even though it allows 'time away'. 'I kept thinking of all that I could have been doing, instead of wasting my time on the course', someone said to me recently.

It is also worth spending a moment on the distinction between education and training. The usual distinction made is that eduction is concerned with general development and that training is specific. Thus, education would be said to equip someone with theories and thought processes which may be used to make judgements and act when current circumstances or frameworks change; training, in these terms, would be related to skills to achieve existing tasks. For the purpose of this chapter the word 'training' is interpreted to encompass both of these.

WHAT IS QUALITY?

Today, nearly every organisation lays claim to a pursuit of quality. The problem with fashionable ideas, however good, is that their very popularity results in woolly definitions. Yet, what is this intangible aspect for which we all strive?

If the assumption of the quality gurus is right, that training must be an integral part of an organisation concerned with quality assurance, then the same rules have to apply to training as to everything else which is carried on within the organisation: trainers must be in sympathy with the core values of the agency, they must be able to analyse and specify the task they have to carry out, to develop systems which will lead to a high quality product, and to plan their work and show the ways in which the product can be measured. It is worth spending a moment on the point about being in sympathy with core values, since many people will regard one of the central tasks of training as being that of challenging taken-for-granted values and assumptions. Training is not, and should not be, the separate entity which some people may want to think. There are attractions to being separate from mainstream activities, but in the end they are outweighed by the limits put on the influence of the training unit. For training to be part of a quality system within an organisation, trainers must accept the core values of their own agency, whether they work in-house for a social service agency or for an outside body. The key point is not that trainers have to agree with everything that is a part of current practice, but that they will only be able to work to full effect if they are a congruent part of a wider organisation.

In the end the prime measure of quality is one of outcome: How far did the training lead to a better service? A critical factor in assessing this is that of the outcome for the user. We do not want too many tasks which are characterised by the 'operation was a success, but, sadly, the patient died'. Thus 'quality' in relation to home care or residential care will be concerned with the way in which the work is carried out. If the task involved cleaning a room, then the result will be visible: has the dust been removed? Is the table polished? Have things been put away? In part this relates to an understanding of what needs to be done, in part to knowing how to do it and in part to having the skill to accomplish what is wanted. Thus, knowledge has to be accompanied by skill or expertise. Even this is not enough: there has to be motivation - the worker has to put in the effort to carry out the task.

What immediately becomes apparent when one person is doing a task for another, is that success (or quality) is linked to other factors, in particular to whether the person carrying out the work does so in a way which is satisfaçtory for the person for whom the work is being done. This is of particular significance in the field of social care, for two reasons. The first is the personal nature of much of the work, in which tasks are often intimate. The second reason is that so many of the services which are being provided are the very tasks which have been learnt from childhood as the hallmarks of growing up: being able to control our bladders, to wash ourselves, to tie up our own shoe laces, indeed, being able to manage on our own. There is a high risk that people feel diminished from the fact of being in need of the service, before taking any account of the way that service is provided.

In this area, definitions of quality have to be more subtle and to allow for interplay between factors and people. Two aspects stand out. The first is whether the manner of the worker to the employer is satisfactory - the room may have been cleaned but the worker may have been surly or even offensive. The second aspect is harder to specify: has the task been carried out in the way that the employer wanted? In one study of home care workers, the authors commented:

> Such clients often wished that the home help would not put the client in a position of having to ask for work to be done and instead would remember what was required. They wanted 'somebody as knows what wants doing so as you don't have to ask them to this and that
>
> Sinclair *et al.*, 1988, p.91

They concluded that three dimensions of home help performance were of practical significance for clients: practical task competence; professional concern; and reliability. Thus, a start may be made on defining quality in individual pieces of work.

The notion of a 'quality service' as distinguished from a single piece of work which is of high quality, is that the level of quality is maintained throughout. There is a move away from a situation where some workers are identified as 'good' and some not, to one where there are known standards and all workers adhere to them.

THE CHARACTERISTICS OF QUALITY

The characteristics of quality have been developed more

fully elsewhere (Clough, 1990, pp.173-207). A quality service is one in which there is a worked-out or conscious approach: current assumptions are questioned; existing structures are analysed; options are considered. The result is that 'knowledge provides the freedom to develop one's own perspective' (Clough, 1990, p.175).

There has to be clarity as to the task both of the agency (or a section of it) and of the individual worker. Without this it is impossible to examine effectiveness. Even with a clear definition of task it is not easy to establish criteria of indicators which reliably show whether the task has been achieved. Yet, the ability to measure remains an essential.

If the key task is that of outcome for users, there has to be a pervading value that people, both users and staff, matter. As with anything else to do with quality, whether or not people think and feel that they matter is demonstrated in the detail of daily events: whether telephones are answered, messages responded to, people do what they say and so on. This is likely to happen only when the worker wants to offer a service: when that is the case, people will feel welcomed, and thought is likely to be given to ways in which the service is more accessible and more responsive.

A high quality service will be one in which the workers have appropriate expertise. The ability of the worker to make relationships is important but is no substitute for skill. We want more than a good bedside manner from our doctor. In addition, if users are to play a bigger part in service provision and assessment, a central feature of what is fashionably called empowerment, it is essential that they have fuller information about:

(i) the criteria for service provision;
(ii) the options which are available to them; and
(iii) their rights, for example in terms of attendance at decision making meetings, the contract for the service which they are getting and ways in which they may question or complain.

In relation to the overall system, quality is perhaps best indicated by whether staff believe in the worth of what they are doing and the value of the product which they produce.

This is more likely to be the case in settings where there is a drive to get things done and to overcome obstacles, when staff have responsibility for their work in line with core values or stated procedures, when there are speedy ways to get resolution of problems and when there is support for staff.

How is a quality service established and maintained? There are three components: line management; inspection; and training. It is essential that 'quality' is not thought to be the domain of one part of the organisation but to pervade all parts. Having defined some of the characteristics of a quality service, these can now be related to the task of training, the focus of the remainder of this chapter. There are two inter-related themes: the contribution of training to improving the quality of the product and, secondly, what represents quality in training activity.

THE PLACE OF TRAINING

A colleague described a lecture he had attended in dismissive terms: the slides used for the overhead projector were poorly produced in that they were difficult to read and had too much to absorb, there were no accompanying hand-outs and the whole was poorly presented. The style of presentation led him to judge that the lecturer had not prepared the material well enough, which he found insulting given the time and expense of travelling to the conference. Attention to detail is an important indicator for any of us.

Determining priorities for training For training to be effective, an agency has to work out priorities. This is best done against the backcloth of a staff and an organisational audit. The staff audit is a comprehensive review of the present state of staffing competence, together with an appraisal of staffing wants and needs. It builds a cumulative picture from individuals. The second aspect, the organisational audit, is the listing of the current training needs of the organisation, for example aspects of the Children Act 1989, of equal opportunities and anti-discriminatory practice, or of the career development of residential staff. Building on these two perspectives, the priorities for the organisation may be set.

A recent synopsis of the state of development of training for care staff included, amongst other issues, the 'ad hoc' nature of much training.

> Training is rarely developed systematically against agreed or stated care practice objectives, which themselves may not exist. Consequently selection of training goals, contents, methods etc., where made, is often arbitrary, unrelated to real practice issues, and takes on a 'flavour of the month' approach. This clearly makes ineffective use of scarce and precious time and resources.
>
> (Payne, nd)

In one way or another a statement has to be produced of priorities in training, hopefully against a staff and organisational audit and with an explanation of the reasons why some things are put in and others left out.

The National Institute of Social Work (NISW) paper referred to above as part of the DoH 'Caring Homes Initiative' cites a range of other issues which may impede training: marginality; organisational difficulties in setting up; uneven use of training materials; lack of criteria for evaluation; lack of information about training opportunities; separation of training and practice. To these could be added the uneven spread of training amongst staff. Consideration of these issues raises some key questions, as outlined in the NISW paper:

> How can 'training' become more central, thereby contributing directly and potently to improving standards of care?
> How can a more systematic approach be taken to staff development and training?...
> Can we identify the more effective training methods?

What these questions assume, as does the emphasis on training in the quality assurance literature, is that there is potential in training to achieve certain objectives. What is the evidence that training makes any difference to the end product?

Outlining the key issues, it is important to remember who is commissioning the training, who has an interest in the training and what is expected to be the end product. In part, some of the quoted failure in training lies in conflicting expectations. Training, in addition to the stated aims, may serve so many unstated purposes: a reward for good performance, the means to change poor practice or even to push people out. At times managers may send staff on a training course because they are anxious about their poor performance without making that explicit to the staff concerned.

If there is to be an assessment as to whether training achieves its objectives and represents value for money, then the tasks and expectations have to be stated clearly. Recall the main criticisms of training: irrelevance to the real world (in terms of task, resources or the realities of daily events); too general (in that there is not enough detail for the specific task); the raising of issues rather than provision of answers.

Successful training will make a link between knowledge and practice. The issue is whether the trainer has the skills to help individuals to make the link. It is important for trainers to be aware that there is more than one route to accomplish this move, from knowledge, to understanding and internalisation, and concluding with demonstrable skills in service provision. People differ in the way in which they learn. Skills can be taught and learnt. An organisation which is in the business of quality development must put resources into training.

ANALYSING THE TASK

The National Vocational Qualifications (NVQ) regulations make clear that a candidate has to demonstrate competence. The skill of the assessor lies in ensuring that what is tested adequately demonstrates competence. We move here into the tensions between macro and micro skills.

What we want from people who provide services for us are the right attitude, the skill to analyse the problem and the skill to act on the analysis,. This holds true whether the service provider is a teacher or someone who cares for us when we are ill. The dilemma lies in what can be judged to be reliable indicators of good practice. The same tension exists for managers or inspectors in looking at the work of others. The evidence of the quality of practice is provided by the detail of the work. The consequence is that when one person gives evidence to back up judgements as to the quality of practice, the other frequently considers that the aspect drawn on is too small to support the conclusion drawn. It is the same with training.

If we want to develop a quality service in any area of the work of an organisation, we have to be precise about what it is that has to be done and the systems which will allow the tasks to be carried out. Without such definition, training is developed on very shaky ground.

Some people may learn to develop skills by being alongside another and watching what is done. But for many, that is not enough. There are few of us who learn to play the piano or drive a car by sitting alongside someone and watching their work. At some stage we have to get people to break down what is happening into small parts and learn how to manage those parts. Indeed the same happens for skilled performers, whether actors, musicians or sports players. Many have described how they have reached a level of performance and could only progress when a teacher, often a different person from a previous teacher, helped them to learn a new skill. For a time the process of analysing and working on a single aspect leads to a loss of spontaneity and wholeness. Yet, when the new skill is absorbed into the repertoire, the performance has been improved.

A quality service is, among many other things, one in which users can expect both a large measure of consistency from different staff and high level performance. For both of these to exist we have to be clear about, first, what the service is designed to produce, secondly, the standards which are to be achieved and, thirdly, the indicators of those high standards.

QUALITY IN TRAINING

Having set the scene, it is useful to consider the implications of what has been written for the trainer themselves. For training to play a part in promoting high quality work in an organisation, the training itself has to be of a high quality. So the first task for a training unit is to specify its own values and the ways in which these tie in with the values of the wider organisation of which they are a part. Thus the questions posed in the preceding paragraph have to be asked of the trainers: What is the training designed to do? What standards are to be set? What are the indicators that the training has met those standards?

It is essential that the particular purpose of the training is specified. Training events may take many forms, including for example short courses, longer programme, on-the-job coaching, individual sessions and so on. It is necessary for there to be clarity as to the way in which the content and methods fit into wider and specific objectives of the training. There has to be congruence between the aims of the staff who provide the training and those who hire them. When a course is criticised by participants or agency staff, it has been tempting for the trainers to justify their own work on one of two grounds: either they assume that they know better than other people what should be done or they point out that training has long term objectives and cannot be expected to achieve everything during the event. There is of course a measure of truth in either claim: trainers may be able to take a wider view than agency staff and such a broader perspective may be beneficial for the organisation; and there are numerous occasions when people say that they only realise much later what they had learnt or the way in which they had changed.

Yet training cannot be allowed to slide out of evaluation in this way. Purchasers have a right to know what they are buying; providers have an obligation to work to a brief; consumers should have information as to what they may expect on the training course so that they may measure what they get against what was intended. This section begins with evaluation because unless there are measurable objectives, training will continue its uneasy meander, viewed on the one hand as mystique on the grounds that good teachers are born and not made, and on the other a waste of time, since 'we don't need a training course to know how to bath someone'. Quality in training, an essential in training for quality, demands specificity of both objective and means of evaluation.

Of course, it would be entirely proper for a specification to acknowledge that there are a number of objectives, some of which are concrete and short term whilst others are longer term. The example of bathing, referred to above, allows scope to examine the issue in greater detail. A training event might be designed to focus on a particular aspect of bathing or on a fuller perspective. If we can construct what we consider a high quality bathing service to include, then we can begin to create a syllabus for the course. The following might be included.

- Assessment of an individual's capacity to bath him or herself (including risk if left alone and ability to wash oneself).
- The relationship of core values such as privacy, independence, choice and dignity to this particular aspect of care.
- The consequent adaptation of procedures to match as closely as possible the wishes of an individual.
- Skills in bathing - washing, grooming, lifting, noting of any physical or mental problems, making the environment as pleasant as possible.
- Systems of recording (Are they necessary? How many notes are made in ways which are as open and yet as unobtrusive as possible?).
- Getting feedback on current practice.

Having outlined the component parts, the next stage is to set out the means to achieve them. Some key questions emerge. What are the best ways to introduce people to ideas or to remind them of perceptions which may have become blunted? How are attitudes exposed or modified? In what ways are skills best taught? How is the perspective of the customer to be included? For example, books might highlight some of the traps into which workers may fall, such as two care assistants talking to each other and ignoring the individual; course members might be asked to conduct a survey of residents to find out their experiences of being bathed; a seminar could be held in which members were asked to imagine what it would be like to be unable to bath yourself and what would comprise good and bad systems for bathing a person; observation of a worker bathing someone could be undertaken by a colleague helping with bathing (obviously with the consent of the individual being bathed).

Consideration has, so far, been given to the contents of a programme and possible methods of presenting this programme. The objectives for these are different. They are the goals of the programme taking into account the capacity of staff and the amount of time available directly on the course and in other time freed from routine work. The objectives may be able to be set at the start before any other planning takes place or they may have to be worked out as the basic questions are asked about content and method.

Thus, what has here been termed 'quality in training' demands a realistic statement of what a training programme is expected to achieve, agreement between purchaser, provider and member as to objectives and clarity as to methods. It would be entirely reasonable to acknowledge what are often seen as the side-effects of training; the opportunity to have time away from one's work to reflect and talk with others, the re-kindling of an interest in the job that emerges when an individual member is enthused whether by a lecture or another course member and, on some residential courses, an opportunity to be looked after in pleasant surroundings and to feel valued. It is not surprising that after some training, members talk about having their batteries recharged.

However, quality in training also demands skills of trainers in the use of techniques and adapting them to the requirements of individuals. The physical environment and 'classroom culture' as well as the trainer's personal style towards the groups as a whole and individuals are also important factors. The job is skilful, but it does not need undue mystique.

Training may fail for reasons which are outside the control of the trainer. Nevertheless, deliverers of training have greater chances of success. An earlier section commented on the NVQ analysis of values, knowledge and competence. Each of these now needs to be related to training. The values of the training staff do not have to be identical with those of the organisation which is purchasing the training, though there are problems created if the values of the two groups are not congruent and if the difference between the two is not accepted. Nevertheless, trainers must make explicit core values which underlie their work, for example respect for individuals. 'Knowledge' in this field relates not only to expertise in the subject areas of the course (though that is vital) but also to knowledge of different training methods. Included in this section is an ability to analyse, both in relation to theory but also to the components of practice. Finally, competence refers to establishing the culture or working style of a programme, the presentation of oneself (as do actors and actresses), the structuring of the programme and the use of a variety of methods, in part in response to the way in which individuals work.

The point has already been made that people who are involved in promoting quality in an organisation must themselves work in ways which demonstrate quality. 'Practice what you preach' is a key motto for trainers. Therefore, if it is being suggested that a high quality service is one in which the user is given as much information and control as appropriate, the same must be applied to the training course. That does not mean that course members are to be left free to do what they want; after all the agency is paying for a programme on a specific theme. Rather, within agreed parameters, participants should be involved in making decisions about the way in which they want to work. Nor should the assertion by members of greater influence result in trainers abdicating their responsibility for what happens within the course: when the behaviour or language of members is not appropriate, course leaders have a responsibility to challenge it (in line with the established values of the employing agency).

There are three aspects which may go wrong. The first is that trainers may lose the freshness of what they are doing when they repeat methods on different courses or repeat a course. The second is that they may stop listening to what their customers are saying, interpreting 'customers' in the widest sense of the 'purchasing agency', the people who attend the training course and the service users who are supposed to get a better service as a consequence of the programme. Finally, trainers may become too reliant on certain methods.

Becoming stale

More than with most jobs, training involves a repetition of various discrete events. The cycle for people involved in training students on full time professional courses is much longer than that for those running short courses, but both are cyclical. How do you gear yourself for the start of a new course, when experience tells you that although the students will be new and different, many of the same questions which have been tackled on earlier occasions will be raised again?

I remember, as a student, Mr Lyward suggesting that teachers did their best work when they were struggling along with the pupils to find out the answers (Lyward's work is perhaps best known from Burn, 1957). I do not think that necessarily to be the case, but I do know as a tutor the excitement of sharing new ideas for the first time, and striving to work at the student's question. There are ways to capture some of that excitement in situations when events are being repeated. The first is thorough preparation. The temptation is to rely on what was done last time. One way to avoid this is to look at the minutiae: Who is going to do what and when? Is the slide projector ready? What do we know of the special interests of the course members or the special events that surround this particular course? What worked well last time and what should we change? Could the presentation of the material be improved?

Secondly, it may be useful to allow space for some of the work of the course to be generated by the members. Thus, a course on management techniques could tackle specific themes by drawing on examples from members or could ask them what are the difficulties with which they struggle.

It is possible, thirdly, to expand the repertoire of methods; the same theme may be tackled in different ways. A fourth way is to involve new people in leading some of the sessions. Finally, it is useful to hold on to something else that is gained from experience. Although there are similarities between people and issues on different courses, listening carefully to each person does result in taking their questions and concerns seriously; the result is that the course takes on its own life.

PLANNING THE NEXT COURSE

In conclusion, it is useful to draw together information which relates to the planning of courses. Here, this is listed under three headings: setting the brief; culture, content and methods; evaluation.

Setting the brief

Objectives must be clear and precise, and should relate to content and methods but also to personnel in terms of who is eligible to apply for the course. There also has to be agreement between those responsible for commissioning the programme and those who provide it. The later stages of course planning and evaluation cannot be carried out satisfactorily without precision at this time.

Culture, content and methods

The word 'culture' is used here to describe a combination of ground rules and style. The following questions illustrate the issues: Is the style formal or informal? What are the limits of confidentiality? In what circumstances would a report back be made to the managers or employers of a course member? What freedom is there for course members to plan the programme? What action follows a failure of a member to attend a session or to produce required work? What control does the course leader assume when course members are offensive to one another or to others not present? Is there any form of assessment? Does the course leader provide feedback on performance either to an individual or a group?

There is little more deadening than rigidity in the use of methods. Most readers will have sat through too many sessions described as seminars or group discussion in which no learning took place and no ideas were generated; it had been assumed that learning would take place because a group of people were gathered together. In a similar way, interminable feedback sessions which follow work in small groups could be recalled. Trainers have to determine what is to be achieved and what is the best way of accomplishing the goal. For example, it may be useful for a group to structure a task rather than to leave it open-ended; alternatively, asking individuals to work out their own responses to an issue in advance of talking with others makes it more likely that each person will think for her or himself. Finally, if at all possible, allow space for variety, including opportunities for individuals to use time as they wish: talking with each other on a set topic; reading articles or chapters from books which have been brought by the course leader; watching videos; writing a briefing note for the action that she or he wants to take; brief consultations with course leaders. There is a temptation to think that what has worked well once will always do so or to imagine that the best methods are those by which the course leaders themselves learn.

In relation to both content and method it is useful to plan carefully in terms both of prior work to be done by course leaders and the length of time needed for completion of tasks. Preparation involves detail: sufficient photocopies of materials (including some spares); knowing what facilities and rooms are available (who is bringing the felt pens?); working out with catering staff the type of meals which are wanted and the length of time needed to serve people. Many have learnt the hard way that it is helpful to have some material up one's sleeve in case some exercises do not work out as planned or people want to go in a different direction. Of course, one of the key factors in any shared work is that course leaders brief each other precisely and work out how they will negotiate in public.

Evaluation

Training is expensive: its justification is that it improves performance. The key question is whether it does that. There is no reason why learning cannot be enjoyable, though it is not necessarily improper for it to be painful. Phillipson (1990) poses a series of questions which could be used to evaluate a training package. They could be used to evaluate a training programme. Perhaps the core point to start from is for a trainer to know what she or he would want their course to be judged against. What are your key indicators of success? Phillipson (p.8) asks whether the material is:

> ...sound and accurate; engaging; developmental...; anti-discriminatory; non-patronising, treating learners and trainers with respect; explicit in its value base; clearly articulating and modelling good practice; easy to use; reasonably priced for what it is; good quality production.

Training will play a part in the development of quality services only when it is itself of high quality.

REFERENCES

Burn, M. (1957). *Mr Lyward's Answer: A Successful Experimentation in Education.* Hamish Hamilton: London.

Clough, R. (1981). *Old Age Homes*. Allen and Unwin: London.

Clough, R. (1990). *Practice, Politics and Power in Social Services Departments.* Gower: Aldershot.

Department of Trade and Industry (1989). *Leadership and Quality Management.* DTI: London.

National Institute for Social Work (1988). *A Positive Choice.* Report of the Independent Review of Residential Care. chaired by Gillian Wagner. HMSO: London.

Payne, C. (Programme Director) (nd). *Training for Care Staff Development Programme.* NISW: London.

Phillipson, J. (1990). Evaluating training methods. *Journal of Training and Development*, 3.

Sinclair, I., Crosbie, D., O'Connor, P., Stanforth, L., and Vickery, A. (1988). *Bridging Two Worlds: Social Work and the Elderly Living Alone*. Avebury: Aldershot.

8

User participation in quality assurance: fashionable dogma or professional necessity?

Mike Devenney

This chapter is about issues relevant to a group of people who comprise a significant number of those receiving social care services - people with disabilities. It traces the history of oppression and inappropriate labelling of people with disabilities, the politics of disability and issues surrounding equality of opportunity. It then examines the concept of consumer-led services and gives examples, before moving on to some practical thoughts about user involvement in services and quality assurance.

The author has cerebral palsy. He is a politician and is Managing Director of Changing Images, a disability consultancy.

POLITICAL PERSPECTIVES

THROUGHOUT THE 1950s and early 1960s in the UK welfare and health services became increasingly sophisticated, as did the consumer. These developments were founded on the economic boom during this period and insatiable demand by the public for new goods and services. The mid 1960s brought about the rise of the civil rights movement. First, the black movement in the United States of America struggled against race discrimination. The impetus of this movement spilled over into a new social consciousness leading to a new era of the women's movement and the birth of the disability movement. Running counter to these civil rights campaigns was the increasing professionalisation of welfare and health services, thus alienating many people from the services they needed and wanted. However, in the late 1960s and early 1970s the people and ideas of the civil rights era began to permeate the system causing a feeling of restlessness to creep through the previously self-assured caring professions. The unchallenged 'right' of the professional to decide what a client needed was gently being called into question and the role of the client became a major debating point. In the early 1970s, with the outcome of the Seebohm Report and the consequent restructuring of health and welfare services, the newly-formed departments of social services took on an innovative image with increased public accountability. Much of the 1970s were spent coming to terms with new local authority structures and developing more effective models of service delivery.

The late 1970s saw the emergence of equal opportunities policies in Labour-controlled authorities. This was in many ways the rise of 'metropolitan socialism', which was personified by the Greater London Council. The application of equal opportunities principles was gradually extended to all local authority services. With the publication of the Barclay Report in 1982, the role of clients and their rights was firmly put on the political agenda. It is interesting to note that the Barclay Report spoke about neighbourhood social services several years before any Social Services Department decentralised its services. In the author's view, the link between the development and implementation of equal opportunities and issues of consumer-led services is fundamentally important.

'Equal Opportunities' is not merely a string of moral imperatives. It is a functional prerequisite of planning and developing an economic and effective service network. Without this pragmatic and targeted approach to service planning an authority - in particular a social services department - will embark, willy-nilly, on a course which will progressively disconnect the Council from the real needs of the community, thus exposing the most vulnerable in that community. An integral component of this equal opportunity strategy must be the involvement of the communities in the decision-making process.

Within this civil rights framework and the development of equal opportunities policies during the last 20 years, there has been a growing politicisation of disabled people. This process has taken several forms. 'The Disability Movement' at one level can be defined as the development of organisations of disabled people, run by disabled people, to represent and articulate the needs and aspirations of disabled people. The British Council of Organisations of Disabled People (BCODP) is the leading umbrella group comprising over 50 independent organisations controlled by disabled people and so voicing the views of over 100,000 individual people with disabilities nationally in the UK. Disabled Peoples International is the international counterpart and is recognised by the United Nations. The distinction between organisations *of* and organisations *for* disabled people is fundamental in moving away from the notion that non-disabled people are always in the best position to do things 'for the disabled'.

Secondly, there has been the rise of single issue pressure groups around disability such as the Disability Income Group (DIG) campaigning for a fairer and accessible unified disability benefit system such as exists in Sweden.

Thirdly, there has been a spate of 'conversions' or reformist activity among large charities working for disabled people. The Spastics Society, RADAR, Greater London Association for the Disabled (GLAD) and the RNIB to name but a few are all desperately trying to convince their respective interest groups of disabled people that they too are becoming organisations controlled by the people they purport to represent. Some are quite genuine and are actually taking positive and swift moves to implement change, however, many are not.

Fourthly, the development of disability units and advisors within local authorities has enabled disability issues to be tackled at the frontline and policy making level.

Finally, the political parties have gradually woken up to disability and began to consult with organisations of disabled people. The acid test is whether or not they will listen to what disabled people say and whether or not disabled people can themselves begin to participate in the mainstream political system.

MODELS OF DISABILITY

Over the decades two dominant explanations of disability have reigned, and have shaped service development and been consolidated in numerous sociology books and by academic researchers.

The first and probably the most prevalent is the *medical model* of disability. This model makes several key assumptions about disabled people: for example, disabled people are passive and cannot decide for themselves; doctors and other paramedics always know more about the 'illness' than the disabled person; disabled people are not 'normal'; disabled people need to be categorised by their physical, sensory or learning impairment. This model paints a pretty bleak picture of disability. It invariably centres on the individual as a problem and defines the person by the nature of their impairment. Disabled people cannot really like being what they are. It is not 'normal'. It is clearly medical and all the paramedical sciences have an important role to play in enabling disabled people to lead as active independent lives as possible and to reduce any pain or other symptoms their condition may impose. However, all this must be done in consultation with, and under the control of, the disabled person. In the instance of a young disabled child, proper information of all the options should be available and ideally discussed with a disabled counsellor or other parents.

The second model stems from the above and is the *charity* or *charity or tragedy* model. Nearly all our major disability charities developed as Britain became industrialised. The eighteenth century saw disabled people put in the workhouse and some may still argue we are not really far removed from that now. The late nineteenth century and the early twentieth century saw the explosion of patronage such as the formation of the RNIB in 1868. Charities were generally either developed by wealthy do-gooders or by the churches. Times have not changed very much. The images that charities continue to portray of disabled people are usually a permutation of the following (take any five from seven to save your conscience): pitiful, needy, helpless, victims, eternal children, asexual, incurable, brave and courageous, exceptional, special and in need of care, but most of all they need your money. Current charity advertising has become very sophisticated but the messages are the same. The begging bowl syndrome prevails. Charities prey on fear, pity, shame, guilt, as well as compassion and concern. Negative images of disabled people are presented in order to raise money to provide essential services. The BBC's Children in Need appeal and Telethon are probably the best examples of how young disabled children are exploited. More often than not, disabled adults are white men and it is very rare to see an image of a black disabled woman. Research in the United States has demonstrated that positive images can raise just as much cash.

There are some notorious examples of charity images such as the series by the Multiple Sclerosis Society who depicted an attractive white woman with pieces ripped out of her. Very striking and scary. But how would you feel if you were newly diagnosed as having MS? The posters were withdrawn, only to be replaced by similar imagery. Who controls the major charities and other social care agencies? It is known that very few are run by disabled people or even employ disabled people in senior management.

It is blatantly clear that neither the *medical or charity* models of disability offer any real political or economic understanding of the true issues that act to discriminate against people with disabilities. Since the mid 1980s disabled people themselves have developed what has become known as the *social model of disability*. The basic principle of this model or explanation is that it identifies the disabling factors within our community and does not lay much emphasis on an individual's physical, sensory or learning impairment. The social model identifies three broad areas of our society's structure which form the basis of the majority of the discrimination. These are the environment, society's institutions and people's attitudes.

Environment

For people with disabilities, the present environment is immensely hostile. Public buildings are still festooned with steps, most ordinary homes are inaccessible and even if your own home is accessible, your neighbour's almost certainly won't be. Public transport is virtually impossible for the majority of disabled people; leisure centres and other entertainment facilities such as theatres and cinemas are either inaccessible or do not provide sign language or annotated performances; pavements are littered with obstacles including lethal bollards, broken paving slabs, shop displays, parked cars and the ubiquitous 'hole in the road'. Lighting in public buildings and on the streets is either inappropriate or inadequate for visually impaired people; public buildings rarely have induction loops for hearing impaired people and when did you ever see a public minicom telephone? The list is endless and very often dangerous.

Despite this hostile environment disabled people are supposed to lead an ordinary, integrated and independent life in the community. It is not surprising that this is not the case. People with disabilities are segregated from early on in their lives in accessible, segregated schools; very often forced into communal living situations in residential settings. Getting about to do every day activities becomes a strategic planning operation by using the limited resources of segregated transport systems such as dial-a-ride and taxi cards. Getting a job is made more difficult by inaccessible work places and lack of public transport. A well designed, user friendly environment benefits all the community, from parents with double buggies to elderly people who may not think of themselves as disabled people but definitely experience all the difficulties of a hostile environment.

This cannot be put right overnight. Recent building regulations have made it a legal requirement for all new and refurbished buildings to be accessible. However the quality of environmental design would be improved beyond recognition by proper consultation with disabled people from the start.

Society's institutions

The society which we live in has set up numerous institutions: including central and local government, the legal profession, the police and armed forces, the church and temples, banking and insurance, the family and marriage. There are, of course, many others. A common factor in all present institutions is that they systematically discriminate against many groups, including people with disabilities. Why is it that disabled drivers' insurance premiums are invariably much higher than their non-disabled peers? Statistically, disabled people have fewer road accidents, so if it is not the actual risk factor, what else can it be than a discriminatory assumption. Should people with learning disabilities have the right to have children? No one questions the right of their non-disabled peers until they have demonstrated they are 'not suitable' parents and even then many children live with inadequate parents. Risk taking is an important life experience. It is essential that, in the instance of learning, disabled parents and their children have appropriate support and training provided to ensure that it is a positive experience for all. Being a parent and having relationships are experiences which disabled people are very often not expected to aspire to, let alone achieve.

Attitudes about disability

Even in the latter part of the twentieth century, disability remains shrouded in taboo, fear, ignorance, pity and shame. Disabled people are stereotyped as being brave, courageous, exceptional in overcoming their disability, or on the other hand, victims of tragic circumstance, pitiful and in need of care. If you are a stroppy disabled person demanding your basic civil rights you have a chip on your shoulder or are perhaps not yet well adjusted to your 'sad predicament'. Why can't disabled people be seen just as ordinary, boring, everyday, intelligent, stupid, inspired or fickle as anyone else in our community? But negative attitudes about disability permeate our lives; everything from biblical references of disability and evil to Captain Hook in Peter Pan or Long John Silver in Treasure Island (all of whom had disabilities) to the 'baddies' in the recent blockbuster film for children, 'Dick Tracy'. Very positive imagery of disability our equal opportunity community portrays? Attitudes are learned. All of us learn from what we see, hear and watch. It is time for disabled people to promote their own imagery. Integrated education with appropriate support for all would soon end lots of prejudices - perhaps painfully at first - but it would definitely enrich everyone's life.

WHAT ARE CONSUMER LED SERVICES?

The failure of service providers to develop a coherent and consistent method of service delivery is manifest. The resulting misery and waste in people's lives beggars description. The idea that consumer-led services would help provide a more effective and responsive service delivery model is by no means new. This notion emerged in the late 1960s and has hung around service providers ever since - some may say like a rope around a condemned prisoner.

Here an attempt will not be made to catalogue, compare or assess the various models of consumer-led services that have been tried with varying degrees of success. The service professionals and academics can do that quite adequately. This chapter will give some political context to the problems of consumer-led services and suggest how it may be possible to move forward.

At this point it may be wise to consider how consumer-led services are defined and to consider what the main parameters of the issue are. The 'clients' or 'users' of personal social services departments, for instance, are our consumer group. The 'user' group spans a huge spectrum ranging from families, children, elderly people, to people with disabilities. In fact, it would be fair to say that the user group is potentially all the communities in any service area.

The 'professionals' involved are essentially all the staff resources of the department with particular emphasis on field workers. It must be remembered that these staff are potential users as well, so that the distinction between the professional and the client is somewhat arbitrary and rests upon the rather dubious notion of professionalism based on training, codes of practice and ethics.

In political terms the distinction may be said to rest more upon class and economic power. The services in question include the whole gamut of services provision, from residential care to housing to care for children under five years of age. It should be noted that, in most instances, services do not operate in a vacuum, and that inter-departmental factors are very important and have an enormous impact on the final shape of the service delivered. However, this is an issue in itself and warrants an in-depth examination which we do not have time to do justice to here.

Finally, a definition, or at least setting the parameters, of consumer-led services may help set the scene and help to avoid confusion. In the context of this discussion, consumer-led will be taken to mean the ability of the user group of the service to influence, change, direct or control the policy development of service delivery practices in order to reflect and meet their changing needs more effectively. This may seem a rather open-ended definition. However, this is deliberately so, as consumer-led services must operate on a range of levels and should not be restricted to a narrow interpretation or a single mode of practice.

Political origins of consumerism such as in social services have, in the author's opinion, run parallel with the development of welfare provision. With the advent of the Attlee/Butler welfare ethos there arose a paternalistic bureaucracy which did not attempt to take on board the possibility or the client having a voice. The system knew best, and if the 'punters' received what they needed, why confuse matters? In the immediate post-war era this model became well established and served its purpose. The consumer goods boom had just begun to flourish and the new 'consumers' were just beginning to recognise their needs and their ability to have them met.

Some may say that equal opportunities and, therefore, consumer-led services have become a fashionable dogma espoused by 'self-styled' radical local authorities, many of whom are Labour controlled inner city authorities with complex social and economic dilemmas. At first glance it may appear that giving credence to consumer-led services in this hostile political and social environment would further compound the problems of dwindling resources, increasing demand, high levels of poverty and negligible government support. Would it not be more straightforward and efficient to allow the politicians and the professionals to decide what priorities are to be set and how resources are best allocated? The general ethos of the professional in society already contains a number of unavoidable difficulties. The professional police officer is not constrained by the diktats of the criminal, and the student does not determine the curriculum. Why then support the thesis that social services delivery should be qualitatively and quantitatively determined by the user of the service? If the domain of the professional in social services is to be trespassed by the user, then are we undermining the trained and experienced human resource made available to the department? Are we replacing the objective judgement of the professional with the ad hoc subjective amateur judgement of the client? In the author's view, the care and welfare of the community is too important a matter to be left in the hands of the politician or the professional.

It is suggested here that there is a distinct and vital tripartite division of roles: the rights of the client; the responsibilities of the manager; and the accountability of the politician. If the formula for combining these three roles is ill-conceived there will be disruption in the community. The manager and the politician will have failed, but the client alone will pay the price for that failure. Without the mechanics to provide the community feedback, professional practices and evaluation will be further forced into dogma and jargon - while outside in the real world the current consensus against the performance and value of social services, for instance, will take further hold and increasingly resemble the worst knocking copy of the gutter press. Each lurid distorted story of human tragedy is laid at the doors of the social services departments who have not, apparently, interfered enough when, for the rest of the time, they have interfered too much.

The hidden assumption prevalent among many professions is that demand is generated by need, and that need is only experienced by those helpless sections of the community which cannot help themselves and who are therefore unable to take part in any formulation of policy or targeting of provision. This nonsensical variant of social Darwinism relates to a homogeneous mass of people who are not fit enough to survive without the passive consumption of support expertly supplied by the professional according to the priorities of the politician.

Of course the reality is that there are many kinds of need reflecting an infinite range of historical disadvantage. How can the professionals then assess and exercise their skills without detailed local understanding? This is vital in order to identify the true needs of the community and not those preconceived by training or dogma. And again, without this local community input, how can the politician evaluate priorities? Without the active participation of the users at the point of need, the professional may scatter valuable resources into a void and the politician operate in a vacuum. Without decentralisation of control and information based on mutual cooperation, can the user and professional fully achieve their common goal of having needs met? This raises the question of tokenism. Disabled people, along with other oppressed groups in society, have experienced tokenism at all levels. Tokenism takes all shapes and forms, but three constant characteristics are: it eventually becomes transparent; it always undermines progress; and it takes a lot more effort to win confidence back from the service users when tokenism has been exposed. Beware! Tokenism potentially lurks in all consultation or decision making processes.

Local authorities, health authorities and voluntary agencies are constantly under pressure to formalise their consultation procedures with service users. Their response is patchy. However disabled people have, in recent times, taken the lead and self-organised on varying levels. The Derbyshire Coalition of Disabled People, The Greater

Manchester Coalition of Disabled People and the Nottinghamshire Coalition of Disabled People have all worked closely in a proactive way to improve statutory and non statutory services. The quality of the services developed reflects the quality of user consultation and control. Some organisations such as the Hampshire and Greenwich Centres for Independent Living (CILs) have taken the concept of user participation further and actively involve service users in planning their own services, for example employing their own personal care assistants or facilitators funded by the local authority and/or the Independent Living Foundation (ILF). Thus consultation moves into control of services. The concept of CILs came from Berkeley, California, USA where disabled people have been directly controlling and planning their services since the late 1970s. This philosophy of increasing user consultation and, in some cases, more control has led several local authorities, health authorities and a few voluntary agencies, most notably the Spastics Society, into a programme of decentralising services into accessible community based networks.

As an example, the London Borough of Islington has undertaken a total programme of decentralisation of services. In practical terms this means there are 24 local neighbourhood offices which offer most of the major council services. The major components of these offices are social services and housing. From the client's point of view the neighbourhood office offers a one-stop shop. The council is currently developing active neighbourhood forums made up of elected members of the community and local organisations who will, in the long term, have an increasing say in how services are delivered in that area and contribute to the overall policy-making process. Superimposed on this decentralised structure is a user-group based system of sub-committees concerning people with physical and learning disabilities, people with mental health problems, elderly people, and children and families. These sub-committees are made up of users of their respective services, are given some officer support, and directly input into the main committees of the Council. In addition, there are co-opted members of most disadvantaged groups on all Council committees. Together these three layers of participation provide the council with valuable information and expertise, and at the same time afford the user some degree of autonomy.

This model of decentralisation promotes a number of important principles. First, it allows the user to have some choice in service provision. Secondly, it allows a planned process of consultation to take place so that the differing needs of the community can be equally met. Thirdly, it allows the easy transmission of information between the Council and the user about what services are available. Also it allows the user to inform the Council of specific needs. Fourthly, it allows the basic concept of participation to take place by all on an equal basis. Finally, it allows the users to have some autonomy over how they use the service.

From the service provider's point of view the major benefit must be seen in terms of a more responsive and accountable service. It could be argued that decentralisation offers the only sound managerial and financial strategy for service delivery in the current economic and political climate. If the services are in the community and accountable to the consumer they will have more chance of being protected and improved. In the author's view it must be a practical necessity for local authorities to engage the active participation of the community. Whatever views are held on decentralisation, what matters is that the key to quality is in delivering services which are relevant to the community, and ensuring that the service changes as the community changes.

CONSUMER INVOLVEMENT

Consumer involvement is very often given lip-service, however very little practical action is implemented. In terms of service delivery there must be two essential components of consumer input. First, direct consultation with people with disabilities about all services on offer. This may take various forms such as day conferences or seminars, questionnaires, mobile exhibitions, sample surveys or more formal user committees advising on policy development. This consultation must be an active dialogue not a professional monologue. Service providers must listen to criticism and be seen to act upon advice. They must constantly be challenged about maintaining the status quo.

Organisational and service change is always painful and may require a change of practice or service ethos. Making the service accountable and accessible to the user must be of prime importance.

When considering service standards and quality guidelines, users and other stake-holders must also be involved. This may mean setting up user committees, for instance in residential units whereby they systematically monitor and develop quality assurance indicators and performance indicators that are meaningful in the real world. For example, are the meals in the residential unit what people want to eat, and at a time when they want to eat it? This may seem relatively unimportant but how many of you sit down to your last meal of the day at 5.15pm at the latest? This was the situation in a residential unit run by a well known charity, until the residential unit was reviewed with active participation from the residents.

User committees must be well structured and focused in order to stop the more cynical professionals side tracking them. There is no doubt that if you have a 12 person user group you will get at least 13 opinions about any one issue! However users must be enabled to distil out the important themes and points in any discussion. This may involve training users in terms of assertiveness, confidence building and running meetings. It also means providing support facilities such as accessible venues, transport, materials in large print, Braille and on tape, sign language, interpreters, facilitators and advocates.

Finally and not least, administrative support in terms of minute takers and the consequent secretarial services of distribution of minutes and agenda must be made available. This is where many local authorities have failed. They profess the need for user involvement without providing the practical back-up.

Change does not happen over-night. This is an old cliche

but it is true. Users must be involved from the outset in any service review or quality monitoring process. They must believe in the consultation or involvement. Good consultation and involvement will help determine short, medium and long term achievable targets with appropriate timescales. The best proof of proper consultation is to watch the change actually happen in the way the users and the professionals have agreed. Change in these terms will be less painful and better received from all points of view. Consultation and involvement with appropriate support and training will bring forth a very imaginative partnership of users' and professionals' ideas.

REFERENCES

Ball, W. (1987). Local authority policy-making on equal opportunities: corporate provision, co-option and consultation. *Policy and Politics,* 15(2).

Brisenden, S. (1986). Independent living and the medical model of disability. *Disability, Handicap and Society,* 1(2).

Campbell, J. (1989). *Disability Equality Training.* London Boroughs Disability Resource Team.

Murray, N. (1982). Giving the client a voice. *Community Care,* 16 Sept.

Katan, J. and Prager, E. (1986). Consumer and worker participation in agency-level decision-making; some considerations of their linkages. *Administration in Social Work,* 10(1).

Oliver, M. (1990). *The Politics of Disablement. Critical Texts in Social Work and the Welfare State.* Macmillan.

The Prince of Wales Advisory Group on Disability. *Living Options Guideline for those Planning Services for People with Severe Physical Disabilities.*

9

International perspectives on quality assurance

Huw Richards

This chapter traces some of the roots and traditions of quality assurance approaches on an international basis. The work of Donabedian is examined and that of Lehman and Rosen, and references made to developments in the USA, Japan, Australia and the Netherlands, as well as the UK. The field of mental health is used for purposes of comparison.

THE ORIGINS OF QUALITY ASSURANCE AND NORTH AMERICAN INFLUENCE

Cost containment, pricing, re-assurance and enhancement

AS EARLY as 1905 Ernest Godman, a surgeon at the Massachusetts General Hospital in Boston, USA, suggested what he called the 'End Result Idea'. This was one of the first attempts to focus attention on some specific measure of *outcomes* of health care. This work evolved into the Hospital Standardisation Programme and by 1952 become the Joint Commission on Accreditation of Hospitals (Tresnowski, 1988). By 1990 two states (Pennsylvania and Colorado) had enacted legislation requiring hospitals to make public their data on medical outcomes and the severity of illness. Elsewhere standardisation of treatment has assisted in cost prediction but has also given rise to more accurate patient demands for specific standard treatments.

This review begins by discussing the situation in North America firstly because the cost-containment issue as a promoting factor in the development of quality assurance creates significant historical differences and some current implications for the UK; and secondly because whatever the cultural differences, many of the UK concepts about quality assurance are derived from this source. So far in the brief example given above the notions of 'outcome' 'standardisation' 'accreditation' 'legislation' and 'consumer preference' have already appeared.

The focus of interest in quality in the USA has itself undergone considerable development. In the 1960s it was fuelled by the rapid growth of health care expenditure. The development of private health insurance, Medicare and Medicaid, meant that the financing of many forms of care was undertaken by third parties on the basis of a claim and not as a direct fee for service. The straightforward question being asked was whether the funds spent on the care process actually benefited patients. This concern has not disappeared but has developed a focus on how cost containment measures and fiscal policy affect quality of care. These trends worked in opposite directions: the reimbursement system encouraged the maximum provision of services to patients and a financial claim, whereas measures which specified set costs per case type (as in Diagnosis Related Groups classifications) created an incentive to minimise the volume and therefore cost of services provided.

'Quality' emerged as a potentially independent overarching and unifying concept and approach, and as a key evaluative criterion of service effectiveness. The North American experience shows that this is not some metaphysical notion, but that quality in health and social care services is the sum of the parts of those services.

The emphasis within the quality debate in North America shows two further divergent trends. The wave of interest in the 1980s was concerned to monitor and protect quality on behalf of various groups with the relatively modest aim of preserving quality and preventing its decline as cost containment measures increased. This was linked to the need for public reassurance rather than quality enhancement. The 'enhancement of quality' trend from the 1970s has re-emerged in the USA, and also in the UK in recent years, in connection with the broad aims of the management of change. Not only are these trends significantly different - the ensuring and preservation of adequate quality and the enhancement of quality as part of managed change - neither takes place in a static policy or resource environment.

Some of the anxieties and suspicions sometimes engendered by the introduction of quality assurance programmes reflect these contrasting concerns for preservation and reassurance or enhancement and change. The fear that a quality assurance programme will provide further material and means for cost cutting, or that its promotion of change will challenge existing interests and shift resources and power within organisations, largely at the behest of managers is not an uncommon response to the introduction of quality assurance programmes.

The UK experience of approaches to quality measurement has not so far become as closely linked to means of cost-containment as in some aspects of the USA experience. It is now accepted in the UK that quality is one factor in a field of forces which contains demand elements,

Fig. 9.1 The 'forces' impacting upon quality

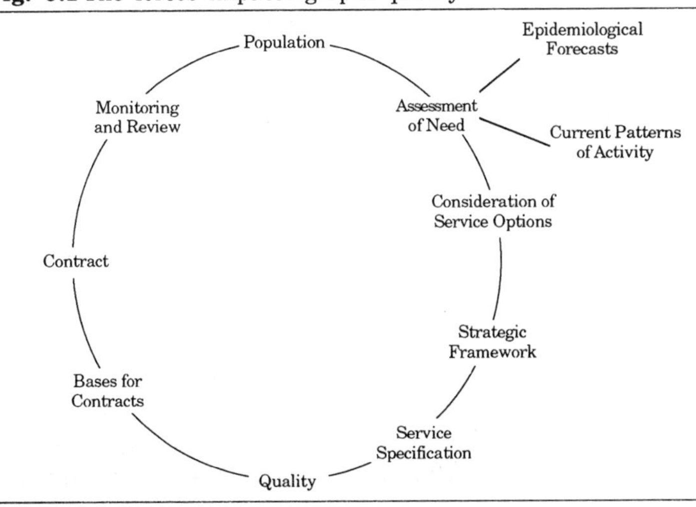

forecasts, needs assessments and in particular *contract specification*. These are shown in Figure 9.1.

Different as the UK social policy and cultural background has been, the UK has nevertheless been ready to adopt some significant concepts about quality from North America.

Concepts of quality

Central to the conceptual debate on quality has been Donabedian (1966). He not only introduced the now almost universally adopted paradigm of 'structure', 'process' and 'outcome' for classifying quality of care studies, but continues to influence the debate. As recently as 1988 in a review of current studies he noted that the term 'quality assurance' is itself a misnomer. In his assertion that quality can be protected or enhanced but not assured, Donabedian reflects the divergent trends between these approaches in the American experience. Donabedian also cautions against a narrow application of the term quality to aspects of services that may be improved by only monitoring structure, process and outcome. He notes that whilst these aspects are of central specific importance the more pervasive influence of professional education, training, certification of competence, regulatory licensure, control of drugs, methods of financing, system design and legal safeguards against malpractice are important to consider.

There are three further significant contributions which Donabedian makes. Firstly the process of quality assessment, the determination of causes for deficiencies, appropriate remedial action and a re-assessment of quality he regards as a never ending cycle. This is significant because it links quality concerns closely to continuously monitored change. This need for continuity and the tendency of services to become inured to less than perfect practice raises the issue of the mix of internal and external features in any quality assurance enterprise. It also reminds us that such continuity will draw upon and refer results back to the central objectives of the service. This will require an understanding of the core principles upon which the service is built and allows a quality assurance programme to make clear the 'value-driven' nature of both care itself and quality assurance exercise. This requires an examination of the principles which underlies both the service being assessed and the quality assurance programme, and presses those concerned with either to be *explicit* about their values and principles.

Secondly, consideration of system design properties which shape the overall direction of care is necessary alongside quality monitoring which aims for fine adjustments. A design fault is a major quality issue.

Thirdly, Donabedian suggests that professionalism is the fundamental safeguard of quality and moreover has the capacity in social policy terms to mediate between, and even revolve, some of the tensions created by a polarity which runs through the American literature as ways to achieve quality: *competition* and *regulation*.

Quality by competition or regulation

The problems associated with competition and its effects on choice, aspects of client purchase and economies of scale by large and fewer providers are noted tensions. Quality is not always determined by literal purchase, particularly when such demand is not mediated by a needs assessment. Fewer providers, which may be the result of competition and lower costs, may in fact drive out choice, and drive down quality. Donabedian notes that there are likely to be 'socially optimal', (that is culturally normative), levels of acceptable quality which may influence the ability of competition to determine quality. Other North American commentators note that following the achievement of common pricing levels that competition itself will shift away from simply costs to demonstrable excellence in areas of clinical outcome (content quality) and customer service (delivery quality) (James, 1989).

Regulation of health and social care is seen by some American writers (James, 1989; Vladeck, 1988) to be necessitated by the pluralist and decentralised nature of such services. Vladeck notes that most approaches to regulation are structural, that is less concerned with processes and outcomes, and that regulatory approaches tend towards a close relationship between standards and costs. Such regulation is less concerned with promoting change and is itself static whilst seeking to evaluate structural aspects of services. These features are directly relevant to current UK experience.

The increased pluralism on the provider side in the UK represents a form of de-regulation, particularly of certain procedures adopted hitherto by local authorities and health authorities as near monopoly providers. The effect of this trend, as in the American context, is to promote new forms of regulation. New Inspectorates in local government (independent inspection units) in the UK have been developed as a result.

Professionalism and health accounting

Donabedian proposes a resolution between the forces of competition and regulation and the paradox that emerges when diversity of provision creates divergence of standards which in turn triggers regulation. This resolution is achieved by maintaining professionalism, promoting professional values, clinical leadership, peer review and self-governance. The UK trends in this direction can be seen in the increased number of Codes of Ethics being developed in nursing and social work, in the development of 'clinical directorates' and in Europe in the development of health accounting particularly in the Netherlands.

In the Netherlands, as long ago as 1980, a national organisation for quality assurance in hospitals introduced a programme which was funded by a fixed charge per hospital bed and used groups of various professionals to produce group judgements on quality and identify the most important cost-effective targets for assessment and improvement. This is an example of structured professional group methods providing the basis for assessing health care outcomes (Williamson, 1988). These internal participative peer and professional approaches to quality assurance have been taken forward in a number of UK systems.

In emphasising the role of professionalism and responsibility as a key to understanding the promotion of quality Donabedian notes, using his own concept of process, the distinction between technical care and the interpersonal process. Since 'acceptability' is a central component of quality as perceived by the patient or client (Maxwell, 1984), the methods of mediating relevant clinical activity becomes significant. Some North American commentators (McGlynn *et al.*, 1988) have noted that, in some methods of treatment in mental illness, particularly in relation to medication adherence, the interpersonal process is itself the equivalent of technical care and can, in quality assurance terms, be observed and validated.

Regulation by litigation and legislation

The existence of 'class actions' and the significance of 'landmark' cases in USA litigation has a significant influence on the use of the law, in the UK, to achieve improved quality of care and service. The technical legal aspects of specific cases were accompanied by a review of statute in a wide number of jurisdictions, particularly in respect of civil commitment of the mentally ill and appeals against such detentions (Curran and Harding, 1978). The willingness of European and Scandinavian countries to review and reform their mental health legislation was influenced by decisions at the European Court and by the World Health Organisation's sponsored review of different jurisdictions. Indeed, material promoting the reform of the English Mental Health Act 1959 was influenced by North American experience (Gostin, 1975).

This recourse to the law by litigation or legislation is the end point of the trend towards regulation of an enforceable kind, and, in the USA context, the consumer 'rights' movement placed emphasis on legal remedies. The influence of the law reform movement and the harmonisation tendency continues in the United Nations Sub-Commission on Human Rights (Steel, 1991) and represents an important foundation for a set of principles and general legal code for mental health legislation and, ultimately, access to and quality of services.

However the operational impact of law reform depends, at the individual level, on some default penalties for non compliance by the provider. Also the patient's 'rights' movement has had a somewhat different impact in the UK context than in the USA. In the UK context statutory rights to services of any quality are a response by those with discretionary duties and are often resource determined. In that sense legal reform as regulation has an important but nevertheless diluted influence on quality of services delivered.

The consumer movement and its impact on quality assurance

The 'consumer' movement in the USA has had a significant impact on the UK, European and Australasian scene. The notion of 'separatism' by patients as opposed to 'partnerships' with professionals and the development of client run services (Chamberlin, 1978), and the self-help movement (Camden Consortium, 1988) has had a major impact on advocacy schemes in psychiatric hospitals (Netherlands), in cooperative Employment Programmes (Italy) and in treatment expectations in psychiatric hospitals (England). The movement not only provided a greater range of services and support systems but has created the conditions within which the consumer satisfaction and patient consultation on aspects of quality assurance programmes can now develop in a cooperative way and minimise purely adversarial posturing.

Three examples of such developments can be given. Firstly, a study conducted in the USA in 1985 which included contact with 450 residents in 105 homes (National Citizens Coalition for Nursing Home Reform, 1986). Seventeen residents presented the findings to a symposium. The resulting publication, *A Consumer Perspective on Quality Care: The Residents Points of View* , an example of the process of consultation, contained proposals for reform and significantly changed the regulation and inspection of homes. The report emphasised 'the need for surveys to measure the actual quality of care residents actually receive rather than the capacity of the facility to provide care'.

The major proposals contained in the report were:

- open lines of communication at all levels of homes
- mandatory pre- and in-service training for workers

- an improvement in working conditions
- elevation of residents rights to a condition of participation in institutional decision making
- participation in inspections
- increased access to the home by the local community.

Similar UK developments are the work which has emanated from the Wagner Report (NISW, 1988) and from *Homes are for Living In* (DoH & SSI, 1989), notably the 'Caring in Homes' Initiative.

Secondly, the National Federation of Families of the Mentally Ill in Japan (Zenkaren) sponsored two major conferences in Kobe and Tokyo in 1988. Partnerships of psychiatric patients and professional carers from Canada, USA, UK, China, Japan and New Zealand were invited to present their biographies and experience of mental disorder, public tolerance and use of services. The events were attended by 1500 people, mostly families of mentally ill people and contributed a significant consumer and carer perspective to the developing mental health reforms in Japan.

Thirdly, the World Health Organisation convened a meeting with consumer groups and representatives in the mental health field in 1987 in Manheim, Germany. This meeting produced a range of views which have a significant bearing on issues of quality of life, service, care, treatment, and participation in decision-making and evaluation. Some of the major areas of concern are given below.

- Terminology - the problems of the use of the word 'consumer'; difference between material consumption and participation and receipt of health care.
- The WHO definitions of impairment, disability and handicap and their use in mental health.
- The recognition of the competence of consumers to participate in decision making.
- The assertion of consumer rights, to be empowered, to be represented, to have access to medical records, to be free of stigmatising labels.

The 'Survivors Speak Out' checklist is a powerful qualitative tool in evaluating mental health services and was reproduced in the WHO (1989a) publication, *Consumer Involvement in Mental Health and Rehabilitation Services*. In quality assurance terms this international gathering and the subsequent report represents a significant milestone in the clear articulation of quality issues by consumers.

Quality assurance and quality of life

One of the bridges which connects the information on service outcomes with patients' actual lives is a 'quality of life' measure. The North American influence here is significant, in particular the work of Lehman *et al* (1982) on the quality of life of psychiatric patients in nine domains:

- Leisure/recreation
- Living situation
- Family relationships
- Social relationships
- Health
- Legal and security
- Finance
- Religion
- Work

The application of a relatively simple quality of life measure covering psycho-social issues for patient groups against comparative norms for the population in general is an area of great promise, particularly if it can be linked to and compared with, service outcome data on similar dimensions.

STANDARD SETTING AND ACCREDITATION IN RELATION TO QUALITY ASSURANCE

Significant work in the field of mental health has been undertaken recently in Australia. A Richmond Implementation Research Project considered the ways in which evaluation strategies could be developed for mental health services in New South Wales (Rosen *et al.*, 1987). This was a wide-ranging overview involving wide consultation, surveying practitioners, considering standards of care, a service effectiveness audit and also considered the role of case-registers, scales of functional impairment, and other key parameters such as user satisfaction, burden of care and quality of life.

The creation of a set of standards and the standards themselves were set out in two further publications (Rosen and Miller, 1989; Rosen, Miller and Parker, 1990). These describe the process by which the standards were created. The criterion established for the exercise was that they should apply both to hospital and community; that they should involve service users and reflect local conditions; and that they should be linked to desired outcomes for service users and care givers. The whole package is referred to as standards for AIMHS: Area-integrated Mental Health Services and it is envisaged that such a checklist of services should be available to users at particular stages of their care.

This ambitious project focused specifically on mental health service users but nevertheless relates these services to the local environment. The main headings of these standards are:

A. *Initial contact and assessment*
1. Early detection
2. Adequate assessment
3. Information and explanation
4. Accountability and contracting

B. *Acute and short term management*
1. Early and timely intervention
2. Range of acute intervention settings available
3. Most appropriate setting for intervention chosen
4. Medication and other technologies
5. Improving cooperation with intervention

C. *On-going management and rehabilitation*
1. Existence of programmes
2. Assessment for on-going management and rehabilitation
3. Review and updating
4. Living or coping skills training
5. Vocational programmes
6. Accommodation programmes
7. Individual service-user support case management
8. Services for service-users family and care givers
9. Volunteer services

D. Long-term follow-up
1. Preparedness to follow-up
2. Systems of tracking
3. Follow-up for appraisal of effectiveness of service

A-D Every phase of care
1. Ethical standards/consumer rights
2. Medico-legal status and safety
3. Communication with and consultation of those involved
4. Continuity and consistency
5. Documentation
6. Promoting of values of normalisation, autonomy, mutual respect
7. Improving community support and tolerance
8. Staffing and staff support
9. Service structure, management and planning
10. Service accountability
11. Service evaluation
12. Access to clinical investigation or specialist assessment and training services
13. Counselling and psychotherapies
14. Cultural factors

This 'phased' approach to standards can usefully be compared with an issue-focused checklist used in the planning document for a proposed multi-site consumer participation exercise by the World Health Organisation (WHO, 1989), reproduced for reference in Table 9.1. The Australian work is operationally focused whereas the World Health Organisation approach is influenced by the notion of legal rights and entitlements.

The work of Rosen and colleagues in Australia shows how standards are developed as distinct from rights. In their work each standard is stated in the form of a service process and outcome.

> An example is Standard E II: The service will encourage and provide access to skilled counselling and psychotherapeutic approaches which are appropriately supervised and adapted for use with serious psychiatric disorders, in every phase of care, and are compatible with other interventions which may be necessary for these disorders.

Table 9.1 Proposed checklist for determining standards in mental health care (from WHO, 1989b)

1. *Access to the Labour Market*
1.1 Is there a right to regular work for mentally ill people?
1.2 Is there a right to sheltered work?
1.3 Is there a law obligating employers to employ a certain percentage of mentally disabled persons? Does this operate?
1.4 Is there a right to vocational training and other assistance to obtain (re)employment?
1.5 Is there protection against dismissal for those with mental health problems?
1.6 Are these programmes which are concerned with stress at work for employees?
1.7 Is a mental disorder caused by stress at work considered as an industrial injury/accident for which compensation may be claimed?
1.8 Is there an 'equal opportunities' employment policy operating on gender, ethnic origin and health?

2. *Income Maintenance (Social Security)*
2.1 Do the consumers have access to advice an assistance to obtain the maximum entitlement to income maintenance?

3. *Health Insurance / Disability Registration*
3.1 Does the consumer have access to health services free at the point of delivery and/or are they covered by a health insurance?
3.2 Do the target group benefit from special services, by being registered as disabled?

4. *Housing*
4.1 Is there a law protecting a mentally ill tenant from eviction by the landlord?
4.2 Is there a law promoting housing for mentally ill people?
4.3 Is there any form of 'respite' housing as an alternative to hospitalisation?
4.4 Is there a right to assistance with housing problems (financial and social)?
4.5 Is there a balance between income for housing, other disposable income and care costs? What proportion of a mentally disordered person's income is taken up by housing costs?

4.6 Are there specific provisions available for homeless persons who suffer mental health problems?

5. *Educational Services*

5.1 Are there basic literacy and numeracy facilities of a remedial kind available to the target group?

5.2 Are there training programmes available to the target group?

6. *Transportation*

6.1 Do the target group benefit from free or subsidised travel; and on what basis of entitlement?

6.2 Do consumers and carers receive assistance in attending for treatment and visiting?

7. *Legal Representation*

7.1 Is there legal advice/legal aid for representation available to the target group?

8. *Ethic Minorities*

8.1 Is the target group characterised by a particular ethnic group?

8.2 Is any particular ethnic minority in the site community cover represented in the target group?

9. *Civil Commitment*

9.1 Does the mental health legislation provide for judicial process of civil commitment?

9.2 Are right of appeal and legal representation for appeals available?

10. *Access to Mental Health Services*

10.1 What legal basis exists for the target group's rights to mental health services and what are these?

10.2 What action can a member of the target group take to obtain or complain about mental health services?

11. *Information on Levels of Provision and the Implementation of Statute*

11.1 What 'norms' or indicators of service provision exist for the target group and should ensure local service provision?

12. *Basic Rights*

12.1 Do members of the target group enjoy these basic rights: for example voting, freedom of access to public facilities, right to marry, have children, own property, inherit property, make a will?

The standard is then cross-referenced to other related standards. In this case there are five such references, for example to family and care-giver programmes. This illustrates the close relationship and inter-dependence of standards with intended outcomes.

The standard is further elaborated by developing its 'Rationale'. In the example given above there were five areas of concern, although some standards require many more. Examples of rationales are therapist characteristics; the place of psychotherapy in combined treatments; cautious selection of the modality for serious disorders; and distinctions between a supportive and an 'insight oriented' type of approach.

The standard is then developed in a further selection, 'Indicators', which provides a wide range of applications with reference to the rationale. Such indicators are detailed and cover specific contexts and contingencies such as time contracts, goal setting, review, and adequate safeguards against user stress. This illustrates an important aspect of 'standards': that they are more likely to be adopted if the rationale for their application is clear; that they do not remain as static and abstract statements of principle or intent, and that they can be applied with a clear linkage between process aspects and outcome. Finally they are explicit and available to users in 'respecting autonomy', or 'promoting social integration' (Seedhouse, 1988). Other key components will be professional expert opinion and user, caregiver and public expectations. Rosen and colleagues addressed this normative aspect of standard setting by creating two Reference Panels of up to 20 people, one of health and social service professionals and one of users, families and voluntary organisations. These included coordination of provision for clinical, functional, inter-personal and material needs; treatment and care in the least restrictive setting; expectations of and consultation between service users, providers and families; integration of hospital and community facilities; integration of service users within their local communities; accountability for the deployment of resources; 'user-friendliness' of services and maximising quality of life for users and their families.

There have been a number of successful attempts to set such an agenda, but distinctive in the Australian case is the elaboration and application of the broad areas into standards within a service context and during four treatment and care phases. Task Groups were set up and assisted by prompt lists of standards and were asked to consider how such standards would apply in these phases of care:

- initial contact and assessment;
- acute and short-term management;
- ongoing management or rehabilitation; and
- long-term follow-up;

with a view to considering what components of service need to be in place to ensure and maintain desirable outcomes for both service users and care givers for a minimum of five years.

The development of standards by Rosen in the Australian context can be characterised as an attempt to produce parameters for care. They include many process issues but draw a focus towards the outcomes for users. This generic approach to standard setting across all stages of care, which presupposes a range of skilled professionals contributing to a service, can be compared to standard setting which is focused on a particular profession.

The Psychiatric Nurses Association of Canada (PNAC) (1979) has adopted 15 standards, each of which contain a 'statement' or 'rationale' and 'assessment factors'. The standards cover areas of multi-disciplinary team work, application of somatic therapies, activity of daily living, problem solving and health promotion. A six point Code of Ethics is part of this package. These general standards applying to a particular professional group have a number of disadvantages: firstly they are so internal to the profession that the focus on outcomes for patients as a result of their application becomes less clear; secondly they are too abstract to be capable of operational specificity; thirdly, they tend to promote an exclusive claim for ethical precepts which run counter to a sharing of general values alongside patients (Richards, 1985). Finally they may, in some instances, portray their profession as a closed system with little opportunity for patient-based outcome criteria to act as the 'assessment' or 'rationale' for the existence and application of their standards.

Donabedian's suggestion that professionalism and self-regulation may be a mediating and balancing factor between competitive forces and public regulation needs some careful consideration in the light of two types of standard setting exercises. Rosen *et al.* (1987) used a wide consultation approach including professional experts, and produced *service* standards which challenge professions to meet them, whereas the PNAC standards are of *conduct* which are significantly different in their contribution to both public accreditation and to quality assurance.

Even standard setting exercises as comprehensive as Rosen's have attracted critics. Some point out the dangers of a static checklist failing to promote action. Others that checklists drive out lateral thinking and innovation in the service or that, by adherence to them, professional discretion is diminished. Rosen himself notes the danger that standards are sometimes seen as authoritarian and demanding of conformity. However his attempts to polarise 'traditional' and 'contemporary' standards, the former as having features of directive, 'top-down' nature, which are conservative and implicit whereas 'contemporary' standards are responsive, innovative and explicit, is not wholly convincing. Much more illuminating are the results of the empirical standards setting work which shows that, in steering a course between the tendency of individuals and interest groups to be prescriptive and to display a wide range of opinion and values, a consultation procedure can, if well focused, create a consensus on currently accepted practice and desired outcomes. Thus achieving some features of Donabedian's notion of socially optimal acceptable standards.

The most significant finding of this exercise, given our transcultural perspective, is that normative standards emerge in culturally relative contexts by paying strict attention to the nature of the process of consultation and participation.

Standards are, however, prescriptive. They may tend towards the minimal and will struggle to be optimal. What place do they have in the activities of quality assurance?

Certainly some quality assurance programmes attempt to assure certain standards but quality assurance programmes tend to be more internal organisational activities and somewhat less public, concerning themselves most often with the character of service transactions than with a guarantee of a regular publicly accountable achievement. This long term assurance is the outcome of the relationship between standards and accreditation systems.

Accreditation is a process whereby an external body of experts testifies that a service fulfils and meets certain pre-determined criteria and standards. It may have as one of its criterion that a quality assurance programme is in place. For credible accreditation much depends on the team or national body charged with making judgements, on the participation of the scrutinised organisations and on the guarantee of the achieved standards being publicly known.

In a recent review of standards and accreditation organisations relevant to mental health in USA, Canada, and Australia (Rosen and Miller, 1989) it was noteworthy that the results showed a general existence of standards applying to most disciplines and covering a range of mental health services. However, of the 11 organisations reviewed, only two allowed for scrutiny by users and caregivers, four emphasised outcome criteria, five produced minimal rather than optimal standards and finally most (seven) did not rely on observation of actual practice and service delivery. It would be possible to apply similar criteria to a range of UK bodies undertaking accreditation, in particular the Royal College of Psychiatrists and the United Kingdom Central Council for Nursing, Midwifery and Health Visiting, and even to the function of registration of residential care homes and nursing homes by local authorities and health authorities.

From this review of some aspects of accreditation it can be noted that quality assurance may be included as a structural and process requirement but that it differs significantly from accreditation in respect of observation of practice, being concerned with enhancement and change rather than minimal or optimal standards, and has more participation by users, families and care givers.

CONCLUSION

This brief review of some selected international trends in quality assurance has shown that the issue of quality, language about quality and the activity commonly referred to as quality assurance takes place within a context that includes the following.

- National legislation, personal litigation and the rights of patients and clients
- Fiscal regulation, competition and contract specification
- Professional regulation
- Accreditation and standards setting
- Consumer advocacy
- Service design

Accepting the challenge that an adequate quality assurance programme will have to take account of these factors, can we begin to see some defining characteristics of a quality assurance programme?

The following list (Table 9.2 overleaf) has emerged from recent UK work with the Enquire System (Richards and Heginbotham, 1992) which was designed in the light of the trends reviewed in this chapter and it attempts to draw a number these features together in a systematic way.

This review has sought to delimit the domain understood as quality assurance and distinguish it from other related activities. The most significant are that quality assurance or quality enhancement concerns participation, dialogue, action and therefore change within organisations.

Table 9.2 Questions which a quality assurance programme should attempt to address (adapted from Richards and Heginbotham, 1992)

1. Does it have a repetitive *cyclical* path and focus on *enhancement* in preference to maintenance?
2. Is it highly *participative*, including users and professional staff to contribute to quality management by increasing *communication*, *shared values* and objectives?
3. Does it take account of user/*consumer statements?*
4. Does it involve *'peer review'* by staff?
5. Is it linked to *standard setting* exercises?
6. Does it involve *observation* of services in operation?
7. Is it *outcome orientated* and does it explore causal links with service structures and processes?
8. Can it compliment but stand *independent* of cost data, and other quantitative data?
9. Is it *action oriented* in applying its findings?
10. Does it embody its *values*, principles and make them *explicit* to participants?
11. Does it have a transparent and *learnable methodology*?

REFERENCES

Camden Consortium (1988). *Treated Well*. Camden MIND. Survivors Speak Out, UK Consumers Organisation, User Action Pack. London: Good Practices in Mental Health.

Chamberlin, J. (1978). *On Our Own. Patient Controlled Alternatives to the Mental Health System.* McGraw Hill.

Curran, W. and Harding, T. (1978). *The Law and Mental Health: Harmonising Objectives*. WHO.

Donabedian, A. (1966). Evaluating the quality of medical care. *Milbank Memorial Fund Quarterly: Health and Society*, 44(2), pp.166-203.

Donabedian, A. (1988). Quality assessment and assurance: unity of purpose, diversity of means. *INQUIRY. The Journal of Health Care, Organisation, Provision and Financing,* 25(1), pp.3-5.

Gostin, L. (1975). *A Human Condition*. London: MIND, National Association for Mental Health.

James, B.C. (1989). *Quality Management for Health Care Delivery*. Report published by Intermountain Health Care Inc., Utah, USA.

Lehman, A.F. et al. (1982). The chronic mental patient: the quality of life issue. *American Journal of Psychiatry*, 139.

McGlynn, E.A. et al. (1988). Quality of care research in mental health: responding to the challenge. *INQUIRY. The Journal of Health Care Organisation, Provision and Financing,* 25(1), pp.157-170.

Maxwell, R. (1984). Quality assessment in health. *British Medical Journal*, 13.

National Citizens Coalition for Nursing Home Reform (1986). *A Consumer Perspective on Quality of Care: The Residents Point of View*. USA: NCCNHR.

National Institute for Social Work (1988). *A Positive Choice*. Report of the Independent Review of Residential Care. Chaired by Gillian Wagner. London: HMSO

Palley, C. (1990). *UN Sub Commission on Human Rights of the Mentally Ill* (draft). Report of the Working Group on the Principles for the Protection of Persons with Mental Illness and for the Improvement of Mental Health Care (H. Steel). Commission on Human Rights 47th Session, Economic and Social Council United Nations. E/CN 44/1991/39 Ge. 91 10275/2816B.

Psychiatric Nurses Association of Canada (1979). *Standards of Psychiatric Nursing Practice*. Winnipeg, Canada: PNAC (Standard XIV reads: 'Psychiatric nursing uses a pragmatic and eclectic approach to the resolution of *nursing* problems'.)

Richards, H. (1985). Social work, professional social workers and the code of ethics. In Watson, D.A. (Ed.) *Code of Ethics for Social Work: The Second Step*. RKP.

Richards, H. and Heginbotham, C. (1990). *Quality Assurance through Observation of Service Delivery: A Workbook*. 2nd edition. London: King's Fund College.

Rosen, A. and Miller, V. (1989). Standards of care for area mental health services. *Australian and New Zealand Journal of Psychiatry,* 23, pp.379-395.

Rosen, A., Miller, V. and Parker, G. (1990). *AIMHS Standards Project* (unpublished). Randwick, New South Wales, Australia: NSW University School of Psychiatry.

Rosen, A. et al. (1987). *Developing Evaluation Strategies for Area Mental Health Services in NSW*. State Health Publication RIQ87-073.

Department of Health & Social Services Inspectorate (1989). *Homes are for Living In*. London: HMSO.

Seedhouse, D. *Ethics, the Heart of Health Care. Ethical Grid*. Chichester: John Wiley.

Tresnowski, B.R. (1988). The current interest in quality is nothing new. *INQUIRY. The Journal of Health Care, Organisation, Provision and Financing*, 25(1), pp.3-5.

Vladeck, B.C. (1988). Quality assurance through external controls. *INQUIRY. The Journal of Health Care, Organisation, Provision and Financing*, 25(1), pp.100-107.

Williamson, J.W. (1988). Future policy directions for quality assurance: lessons from health accounting experience. *INQUIRY. The Journal of Health Care, Organisation, Provision and Financing,* 25(1), pp.67-77.

World Health Organisation (1989a). *Consumer Involvement in Mental Health and Rehabilitation Services*. WHO/MNH/HEP.

World Health Organisation (1989b). *Initiative of Support to People Disabled by Mental Illness*. MWH/MEP/898. Proposal for a multisite project. Annex 3.

10

Total Quality Management (TQM) The way ahead

John B Piggott and Gillian Piggott

This chapter provides an introduction to the concept of Total Quality Management (TQM), and the benefits to be obtained from it. It summarises the major aspects of the work of Deming, Juran and Crosby, briefly traces TQM's history, and includes a number of practical steps to introducing Total Quality Management into an organisation.

TQM provides a process and framework for implementation of a number of the quality concepts introduced in earlier chapters. It requires a total commitment across the organisation (from the very top) to the continuous improvement of services and to the nurturing of a culture which releases the potential of staff and eliminates barriers to improvement in all aspects of the organisation's work.

INTRODUCTION

IF A random sample of people were asked to describe what they mean by 'Total Quality', the chances are that the answers would be very varied. However, in all probability certain manufacturers or organisations are likely to be mentioned. Marks and Spencer, Rolex for watches, I.B.M for computers are all perceived as providing a high standard of product or service. Although they differ in management style and culture, these organisations also have something in common. The public image is of the integrity of the product or service they offer, employees' pride in their work, and the desire to be 'the best'.

The question is: How do you achieve public perception as a provider of high quality products or service? In an industrial situation: by *delighting your customer*.

Many books and articles have been written on Total Quality Management. Most have an industrial or manufacturing background. It may be felt that what can be applied in industry cannot be relevant to Charities, Social Care Agencies and Hospitals. This may be so in minute detail - however, the principles can be used and the techniques extended. The application has to be related to the particular organisation. The authors' experiences in manufacturing/service/health authorities have clearly demonstrated the need for a unique approach to be developed for each organisation.

How it started

Historically, before the production line process was invented, craftsmen were involved in all aspects of the product they manufactured. They took responsibility for their own work, from the initial design, to the finished product.

About the turn of the century, Frederick Taylor (among others) turned his attention to increasing productivity by breaking down the work process into small components (see, for example, Taylor, 1947). Each component contributed to the whole. However, the worker no longer had any involvement with the complete final finished product and rarely met the final customer. Provided the work was carried out to the instructions given, the worker considered he or she had fulfilled the requirements expected of him or her.

In an effort to control the quality of the product, inspection to sort the good from the bad became necessary. This in turn increasingly became a management tool with which to blame poor workmanship for an unsatisfactory product. Not surprisingly, motivation became difficult to maintain.

The initial attempts to involve the workforce were seen

in the mid-30s. Maslow and Hertzberg defined factors needed by employees in order to retain interest in their work (see Maslow, 1943 and Hertzberg, 1966). This resulted in management initiatives as diverse as job rotation and team working. However, no universal panacea was found that could address the problem of individual ownership of work. Some organisations incorporated behavioural psychology concepts into their management philosophy. Today, the research done by the 'founding fathers' into organisational behaviour has been expanded and included in the concept of Total Quality Management.

The TQM initiative recognises the need for all the workforce to be involved with the supply of high standards of work. Whilst the British Standard 5750 quality systems standard concentrates on procedures to control the product or service to the specification, TQM takes the view that quality is not just a matter of good procedure. The culture and ethics of the organisation, together with the attitude of the workforce, all contribute towards the final standard of the goods or service supplied. It is as much about people as it is about the product.

Whatever the organisation, whether it is manufacturing, service, health care or social care, one common factor is the need to provide a consistently high standard of goods or service - or both. Without this, customers will look elsewhere.

There are many reasons for introducing TQM over and above the continuous improvement in service standards which we have come to expect. A major reason is to release the potential of the most important asset - employees. Everyone, when they start a new job, wants to do a good job. However, sometimes something happens which prevents this - maybe procedures, lack of recognition, and so on. This can result in frustration which causes absenteeism, high staff turnover and difficulty in recruiting staff. An effective Total Quality Management approach will have the effect of assisting in releasing the potential of everyone, removing the barriers which exist, and helping individuals to have more control of their own working environment, for the benefit of the Company.

Every organisation has to count the cost of waste, which in service industries often accounts for 30% of operating cost. TQM addresses this factor within any business. In the social care sector, where money is limited, the maximum utilisation of resources is an imperative. Attacking the reduction of waste becomes a vital part of any TQM process.

The need for change

Why was it necessary for organisations to change their approach towards their workforce?

Post World War II saw enormous changes in the workplace. The old manufacturing basis of the developed nations was overthrown by the apparently inexorable march from the Pacific basin. Household names disappeared overnight. Companies that were renowned for craftsmanship and skill were lost, along with the rest.

How did this happen? Were management procedures so old-fashioned? Were Western nations really so under-capitalised and poorly equipped? These questions will, no doubt, be asked for many years to come. What became obvious was the need to change. Traditional methods had to be examined, long held beliefs questioned. The results of this examination has affected the way in which organisations operate.

Foreign influence

To say the Japanese dominate the modern approach to management is not entirely true. However, public perception is that the Japanese influence on methods of manufacturing and motivation have radically changed Western thinking.

Immediately after World War II, Dr W. Edwards Deming, an American expert on quality and statistical control, was invited to visit Japan and help rebuild their shattered industrial infrastructure. Deming's advice at that time was largely ignored in the United States -yet another example of a 'Prophet being without honour in his own Country'! However, the Japanese enthusiastically adopted his philosophy and used it when planning the rebuilding of their industrial base.

Dr J.M. Juran, another American, evolved his own approach, and his influence was evident in the 'Japanese miracle'. Later, Philip Crosby, whilst being influenced by Deming and Juran, evolved his own teaching and set up the 'Crosby Quality College' in the United States to disseminate his ideas.

The American influence on quality philosophy is not always appreciated. However, although the Japanese are largely credited with employing the principles of quality in design, manufacture and service, their own 'home grown' experts are now becoming household names. Kaoru Ishikawa (see Ishikawa, 1982), the statistician Genichi Taguchi, and others have all had an impact on the achievement of high quality standards within Japan.

What of Europe? Does Europe follow where America and Japan lead? It has to be said that, while there are Europeans whose thinking has influenced the total quality initiative, in general the major contributions have come from America and Japan.

THE TQM PHILOSOPHERS

To gain a greater insight into how TQM has developed, it is useful to examine some of the experts and their particular philosophies.

Dr W. Edwards Deming

Dr Deming originally carried out fundamental studies of statistics, particularly the work of Walter Shewhart. He extended this research to quality, and his techniques were well received in Japan after the 2nd World War. The Japanese, desperate to rebuild their ruined industry, were eager to learn the latest techniques. They were also aware that to continue to copy Western manufactured products, as they had done prior to the War, would not create the required economic growth. Copying and shoddy goods were out - quality and innovation were required.

Deming teaches management by positive cooperation, as opposed to management by conflict. He encourages a 'change of culture', which means a management style which positively encourages cooperation, and which acknowledges that it is the customer's perception that counts. Deming has said:

> It will not suffice to have customers who are merely satisfied. An unhappy customer will switch. Unfortunately, a satisfied customer may also switch, on the theory that he could not lose much and might gain. Profit in business comes from repeat customers, customers who boast about your product and service are customers who recommend you to their friends.

Deming has produced a list of 14 'Points for Management' to help understand and implement his way of thinking. He emphasises that this list (see Table 10.1) is not absolute, but will adapt and change according to the requirements of the time and the organisation.

Table 10.1 Deming's points for management

1. **Constancy of purpose** Create constancy of purpose for *continual improvement* of products and services.
2. **New philosophy** Adopt the new philosophy for economic stability. Create a partnership with your customer and ensure that the customer is *delighted with your performance.*
3. **Ceased dependence on inspection** Eliminate the need for dependence on inspection by introducing *prevention not detection.*
4. **End lowest tender contracts** Consider the overall cost to your business of having a supplier whose *delivery, quality and stability you can depend on.*
5. **Constantly improve systems** Search continually for problems, *continually improve the systems* of production and service and every other activity in the business.
6. **Institute training** Institute modern *methods of training* and re-training, on and for the job.
7. **Institute leadership** Institute modern methods of supervision - leadership - focusing on *helping people and machines* to do a better job.
8. **Drive out fear** Encourage effective two-way communication and use every means possible to drive out fear throughout the organisation.

9. **Break down barriers** Break down barriers between departments and levels of staff. *We all work for the same organisation.*
10. **Eliminate exhortations** Eliminate the use of slogans, posters and exhortations.
11. **Eliminate targets** Eliminate work standards that prescribe arbitrary numerical quotas and targets. *Do we pay just for quantity, not quality.*
12. **Permit pride of workmanship** Remove barriers that rob hourly-paid workers and people in management of their right to pride of workmanship. *Let people contribute to their working environment.*
13. **Encourage education** Institute a vigorous programme of *education and encourage self-improvement* for everyone.
14. **Top managements' commitment** Clearly define top management's *permanent commitment to ever-improving quality* and productivity.

Deming has drawn the following conclusion:

> Who will survive? Companies which adopt constancy of purpose for quality, productivity and service, and go about it with intelligence and perseverance, have a chance to survive. They must of course offer products and services which have a market. Charles Darwin's law of survival of the fittest and that the unfit do not survive holds good in free enterprise as well as in natural selection. It is a cruel, unrelenting law.
> The problem will solve itself. The only survivors will be the companies with constancy of purpose for quality, productivity and service.
>
> (*Society of Motor Manufacturers and Traders Tools and Techniques for Quality Management,* 1991)

Dr J.M. Juran

In Japan the influence of Dr Juran, an American, has been recognised by the award of the prestigious Order of the Sacred Treasure. Like Dr Deming, Dr Juran was initially a statistician who recognised that knowing the technical aspects of quality did not help to manage and achieve quality. He advocated that achieving quality had to be through communication, management and people.

Juran details three basic steps to quality improvement:

- structured annual improvement plans;
- massive training programme involving the whole workforce; and
- senior management leadership.

Like Deming, he maintains the majority of quality problems are systematic and therefore the responsibility of management.

It is interesting that Juran is strongly against 'campaigns to motivate the workforce to solve the company's quality problems by doing perfect work.' In his view slogans and motivation alone 'fail to set specific goals, establish specific plans to meet these goals, or provide the needed resources.'

Juran relates quality control on company-wide quality management to the systematic methods used to meet business or financial goals. He talks of a 'trilogy' of basic managerial processes through which to manage quality. He compares his quality trilogy with financial terminology:

Trilogy Processes	*Financial Terminology*
Quality planning	Budgeting, business planning
Quality control	Cost control, expense control inventory control.
Quality improvement	Cost reduction, profit improvement

Juran's systematic approach to quality management covers the following:

- Establish policies and goals for quality
- Establish plans for meeting these quality goals
- Provide the resources to evaluate progress against the goals and take appropriate action
- Provide motivation to stimulate people to meet the goal

Like other quality philosophers, Juran (1988) has provided a quality road map (Table 10.2).

Table 10.2 Juran's quality planning road map

- Identify who are the customers
- Determine the needs of these customers
- Translate these needs into our language
- Develop a product that can respond to those needs
- Optimise the product features so as to meet our needs as well as the customers's needs
- Develop a process which is able to produce the product
- Optimise the process
- Prove the process can produce the product under operating conditions
- Transfer the process to the operating forces

Philip B. Crosby

Philip Crosby began his career as an inspector on the factory floor. This practical background has influenced his approach, which has been described as evangelistic. The essence of Crosby's teaching is contained in the 'Four Absolutes of Quality', and in a 14-step process of quality improvement (Crosby, 1979; 1984). At the root of his concept is his continued admonition that the job of management is 'To help people'. This is at the heart of the TQM movement.

Crosby argues that to manage quality you must have the following.

- A *definition* for quality that can be readily understood by all. The start of a common language that will aid communication.
- A *system* by which to manage quality.
- A *performance standard* that leaves no room for doubt or fudging by any employee.
- A *method of measurement* which will focus attention on the progress of quality improvement.

This list of attributes leads to the 'Four Absolutes' that Crosby outlines for managing quality (Table 10.3).

Table 10.3 Crosby's 'Four Absolutes' for managing quality

1. **The definition** Quality is conformance to requirements, not goodness.
2. **The system** Prevention, not appraisal.
3. **The performance standard** Zero defects: not 'that's close enough'.
4. **The measurement** The price of non-conformance to requirements (cost of quality) not quality indices.

The Crosby methodology for implementation is contained within the 14 step quality improvement process (Table 10.4).

Table 10.4 Crosby's quality improvement process

	Implement	*Purpose*
1.	**Management commitment**	To make it clear where management stands on quality.
2.	**Quality improvement team**	To run the quality improvement programme.
3.	**Measurement**	To provide a display of current and potential non-conformance problems in a manner that permits objective evaluation and corrective action.
4.	**Cost of quality**	To define the ingredients of the cost of quality, and explain its use as a management tool.
5.	**Quality awareness**	To provide a method of raising the personal concern felt by all personnel in the company towards the conformance of the product or service and the quality reputation of the Company.
6.	**Corrective action**	To provide a systematic method of resolving forever the problems that are identified through previous actions.
7.	**Zero defects planning**	To examine the various activities that must be conducted in preparation for formally launching the Zero Defects programme.

	Implement	*Purpose*
8.	**Employee education**	To define the type of employee training that is needed in order actively to carry out their part of the quality improvement programme.
9.	**ZD day**	To create an event that will let all employees realise through a personal experience, that there has been a change.
10.	**Goal setting**	To turn pledges and commitments into action by encouraging individuals to establish improvement goals for themselves and their groups.
11.	**Error-Cause removal**	To give the individual employee a method of communicating to management the situations that make it difficult for the employee to meet the pledge to improve.
12.	**Recognition**	To appreciate those who participate.
13.	**Quality councils**	To bring together the professional quality people for planned communication on a regular basis.
14.	**Do it over again**	To emphasise that the quality improvement programme never ends.

In the authors' opinion, these 14 steps do not fit all national or even all company cultures. However, if treated as guidelines, they can be considered as a tool towards initiating quality improvements.

Dr Kaoru Ishikawa

Dr Kaoru Ishikawa is probably one of the better known of the Japanese contributors to the theory of quality management. He is the originator of the Ishikawa cause and effect diagram, sometimes known as the 'fishbone' diagram. This approach to problem solving is widely followed in the West.

Dr Ishikawa recognised the benefits of involving everyone in the company and outlined some of the tools which should be used (Ishikawa, 1982). Table 10.5 gives some examples of these tools.

Table 10.5 Examples of basic tools

1.	Check sheets	**Record data in a structured way**
2.	Histograms	**Show spread of data**
3.	Pareto	**To rank problems**
4.	Cause and effect diagrams	**Show relationship of probable causes and their effect**
5.	Scatter diagrams	**Show relationship between paired data**
6.	Control charts	**Evaluates process variability**

Total Quality Management has not developed solely through the efforts of the above philosophers. However, their influence has been of major importance. Whilst it is acknowledged that many others could claim recognition in the quality field, space prevents a detailed history of all those who have contributed to TQM - the bibliography may help with this.

HOW TO GET STARTED

How do *you* select the right approach to TQM for *your* organisation? Before this can be done it is necessary to look at what is meant by Total Quality Management, and what is intended to be achieved.

TOTAL This means that everyone in the organisation has to be involved in the improvement process, from the Chief Executive to the people working in the offices/workshops/ wards, and in every department and activity across the organisation.

QUALITY There are many definitions but the authors' preferred one is:

> Delighting the customer by continuously meeting and improving upon agreed requirements
>
> (Macdonald and Piggot, 1990)

This has the advantage of being binary. There is a clear requirement which has to be met, but there is also a recognition of the need to continuously improve, in order to 'delight' your customer.

MANAGEMENT The improvement process will not happen by accident. It has to be planned and must involve people, facilities and processes. Therefore, it has to be managed.

The organisation is composed of numerous inter-related functions. To be successful, the input and output of each process must be clearly defined, together with a detailed requirement.

An effectively managed TQM process will break down the barriers to communication which exist within the traditional departmental structures; the process helps people co-exist, and recognises that they are both customers and suppliers within the same organisation. Work is a succession of processes which are dependent upon each other. The desired outcome is that the end customer can be not just satisfied with the product/service, but delighted.

TQM exists to change the traditional communication networks to a culture in which everyone feels free to become involved, in order to meet the objectives of the business. It means changing management behaviour and the attitudes of people working in the organisation.

Total and continuous improvement (the objective of the TQM process) insists that everyone can share and understand the purpose, principles and values of the organisation. With this must go the shared knowledge of how to improve by the use of quality improvement systems and tools.

There are differing views put forward by the experts on which approach to TQM to select. Tom Peters, in his book *Thriving on Chaos* (Peters, 1988) stated 'that most quality programmes fail for one of two reasons: they have a system without passion or passion without system. You must have both. The question was developed as to which system you should follow: for example, Deming, Juran, Crosby, or invent a system of your own. He then went on to say

'Eventually you will develop your own scheme if you are successful. But I strongly recommend that you do not begin with a Chinese menu. Pick one system and implement it religiously.'

In the authors' opinion, based on implementing quality across manufacturing, service, health care, for success to be achieved, there are six stages in the quality improvement process which lead to continual improvement. It is essential that the improvement becomes a *process* and is not a programme, which has a start and a finish.

The six stages of quality improvement (Macdonald and Piggott, 1990) are given below.

1. Assessment and awareness
Assessment of the company's need for quality improvement: of waste; of customer satisfaction; of employee attitudes; executive decision to change; communicating the need to change.

2. Organising for quality improvement
Establishing the quality management organisation: executive definition of objectives, policy, principles and values; establishment of the quality element of the business plan; establishing criteria and benchmarks to measure the process and resultant implementation.

3. Education
Educating and training all: providing competence in analysing work processes, measurement and process improvement. Focused on driving out fear, breaking down barriers and statistical thinking.

4. Establishing stable processes
Management-led analysis of key work processes: establishing customer, process and supplier requirements; establishing independent reviews for all products or services; implementing a company-wide improvement system; eliminating major problems.

5. Total involvement of all employees
Introduction of measurement by all work groups: establishing formal recognition; removing barriers to open communication; introduction of group-set goals in work groups.

6. Continuous improvement
Further analytical and statistical training of facilitators, managers and key employees: widespread use of statistical methodology; planned reduction of variation in all processes; introduction of other sophisticated tools; the whole organisation involved in Kaizen; continuous improvement of the process.

MAKING IT HAPPEN

In order to make continuous improvement happen within the organisation, the following approach may be helpful. This is based upon experience of implementing quality initiatives in both the private and public sectors. Further details are developed in Macdonald and Piggott (1990).

The phases which need to be covered are discussed below.

Awareness and assessment

For the improvement process to be successful it is essential that the entire management team from the very top are actively involved. Therefore, an awareness session should be arranged by the Chief Executive and led by someone who has knowledge and experience in implementing TQM. This level of expertise would normally have to be found outside the organisation.

The objective of the awareness session is to get agreement from all concerned of the need to change, to ensure that senior management understand the concepts of TQM and what is involved, and take ownership of the improvement process. It is vital that the Management team have a knowledge of what they would like their organisation to become and where they currently stand.

In order to develop an improvement strategy, it is essential that an assessment is carried out, to determine where they are and where they need to be. This assessment should include employee attitude surveys, perception of supplier/customer relationships and areas of waste within the organisation.

On completion of the assessment, the management team

should recognise the need for improvement and lead the improvement process by undertaking the following.

- Defining the constant purpose of the organisation and the improvement principles and values.
- Ensuring that there is a continuous programme of education and self-improvement for everyone.
- Removing all the barriers that prevent quality being achieved through people.
- Providing the necessary resources.
- Ensuring that their actions demonstrate the integrity of the continuous improvement process.

Planning

This is a vital stage in the implementation of the improvement process and has a significant effect on its success. A plan to cover the initial implementation activity, which is then incorporated into the organisation's strategic business plan, should be developed. Quality must become part of the normal business planning activity. The initial plan must include three factors to make it happen:

(i) provide the environment;
(ii) provide the process; and
(iii) provide the support.

As management are the only people who can make it happen, they must be actively involved throughout. Management, by accepting the need for change, have the power to create the environment where TQM can succeed.

Provide the environment

The key factors in providing the environment are the development of mission and a vision of where the company/organisation should be. This is then supported by principles and values, to which everyone in the organisation can relate, in order to achieve the mission.

A key point in providing the environment is to create a common language for quality which everyone can understand and relate to their part in the improvement process. Every organisation has to develop its own definition of quality, to suit it's own environment. An example of such a statement is given in Table 10.6, and was developed by St. Helier NHS Trust. This was one of the fiirst self-governing Trusts formed in April 1991; it decided to respond posiitively to the challenge of the NHS reforms and its new structure. Their definition of quality is:

> Pleasing our patients, clients and colleagues by continuously meeting and improving upon agreed requirements.

The St. Helier Trust then went on to develop their Mission Statement, Quality Policy and Principles and Values. These are printed in full, and are those areas which they considered to be of prime importance to providing a quality service.

Table 10.6 The Mission Statement and Policies and Principles developed by St Helier NHS Trust

Trust Mission

The purpose of the Trust is to respond to individual patient needs.

- We will achieve this by offering a comprehensive range of specialised health care services.
- We will continuously improve the quality of our services.
- We will be a progressive employer by enabling staff to realise their full potential.
- We will provide a high level of medical and professional education.
- We will grow by providing quality services to an increasing number of patients.

Trust Quality Policy

- We will identify and respond to the health needs of each of our patients and strive to exceed their expectations of us.
- We recognise that the special nature of health care requires each individual to carry out their duties conscientiously and without delay.
- We will further improve our service by continuous review and critical evaluation of our work.
- We will fully understand the requirements of our jobs and will conform to them and our professional requirements at all times.

Trust Principles and Values

We are dedicated to the relief of ill health and improved well-being of our consumers of health care whether we call them patients, clients, users, residents etc. This is achieved through a partnership with them, their doctors and their health authorities.

- We will treat our patients with dignity, courtesy and respect.
- We recognise that each person is a unique individual whose needs are physical, emotional, spiritual and social.
- We will protect the confidentiality of our patients' personal matters at all times.
- We will honour our patients' rights for information, explanation and participation in their care process.

The Trust is dedicated to the success of its service and recognises that its Mission can only be achieved through people. Therefore:

- We all have a responsibility towards providing a quality service.
- We will each commit ourselves to continuous self-development.
- We will recognise individuals for their contribution.
- We will communicate with each other in an open and frank manner.
- We recognise that all our people want to do a good job and need to know exactly what is expected of them.
- We will treat each other with dignity and respect.

The Trust Executive Board is committed to continuous improvement and leadership by:

- Defining the Mission, Quality Policy and Principles and Values of the Trust.
- Ensuring that there is continuous education and self-improvement for everyone.
- Removing all the barriers that prevent improvement and open communication being achieved.
- Creating an environment that will enable our staff to make their maximum contribution to the care of our patients.
- Ensuring that all their actions uphold the Principles and Values of the Trust.

The foregoing illustrates the statements developed by a major NHS Trust to lead them forward. This was a group of people who, by their nature, are very caring, and have pride in their work. Each organisation must develop their own statements, but everyone can learn from one another. It is not necessary to re-invent the wheel.

Another example of writing principles and values is given in Table 10.7.

Table 10.7 Principles and values for planning TQM.

Company Principle

Maintaining an international viewpoint, we are dedicated to supplying products of the highest efficiency yet at a reasonable price for worldwide customer satisfaction.

Management Policy

1. Proceed always with ambition and youthfulness.
2. Respect sound theory, develop fresh ideas and make the most effective use of time.
3. Enjoy your work and always brighten your working atmosphere.
4. Strive constantly for a harmonious flow of work.
5. Be ever mindful of the value of research and endeavour.

Where did the information in Table 10.7 come from? Can you relate to any part of it? It came from a major world class Company, 'Honda', and apparently was initially prepared by the founder.

The development of these types of statements are the first steps towards introducing TQM, as they clearly define the type of organisation required.

A number of social care agencies have already embarked upon this course of action through the design of mission statements and quality assurance policies. For example, The Spastics Society, after wide consultation with staff, service users, parents and carers of people with disabilities and other stakeholders, produced the statement given in Table 10.8.

Table 10.8 The Spastics Society's quality assurance policy

Statement of our beliefs and mission
The Spastics Society is a voluntary organisation active across England and Wales.

Our beliefs
We believe that every individual has a right to control his or her own life and to share in the opportunities, enjoyment, challenges and responsibilities of everyday life.

We believe that care and concern for each and every person and respect for their human rights is central to any caring community.

We believe that people with a disability are handicapped by the attitudes of others, at home, in the community, at work, and in national and local government.

Our purpose
We exist to enable men, women and children with cerebral palsy and associated disabilities to claim their rights, lead fulfilling and rewarding lives and play a full part in society.

We shall achieve this purpose through a wide range of activities and services which respond to individual needs, choices and rights.

Our services and activities will include creating housing, education and employment opportunities; expert and loving care; support for families and carers; research; advocacy, information and advice services; support for self help groups; campaigning and other activities designed to change public behaviour.

Making it happen
Money gives us the power to make things happen.

We aim to win widespread and generous financial support from all parts of society.

We aim for the highest standards of financial and service management.

People are central to our success. This stems from the experiences of the people who use our services and the contribution of those who work and volunteer for us.

We expect the highest standards from our staff and volunteers: complete honesty and integrity, total professionalism and a commitment to the people whose interests we exist to serve.

We seek to recognise good practice, and encourage creative and innovative work. We are committed to establishing equality of opportunity for all and to the professional development of all our staff and volunteers.

This statement expresses our core beliefs and aims.

Our plans for our future will flow from what we have expressed here.

We are committed to quality in all our services and activities.

We will therefore constantly monitor, evaluate and seek to improve our services further in accordance with stated beliefs and aims.

Provide the process

Once the environment has been established, it is then necessary to provide the structure, systems and education to implement the process of continuous improvement. All work is a process, and there will always be ways in which this process can be improved, irrespective of the type of work being undertaken.

STRUCTURE

The first step is to ensure the process works effectively by having the necessary structure in place to implement the quality initiatives. A typical organisation is shown in Fig.10.1.

Fig 10.1A typical organisation

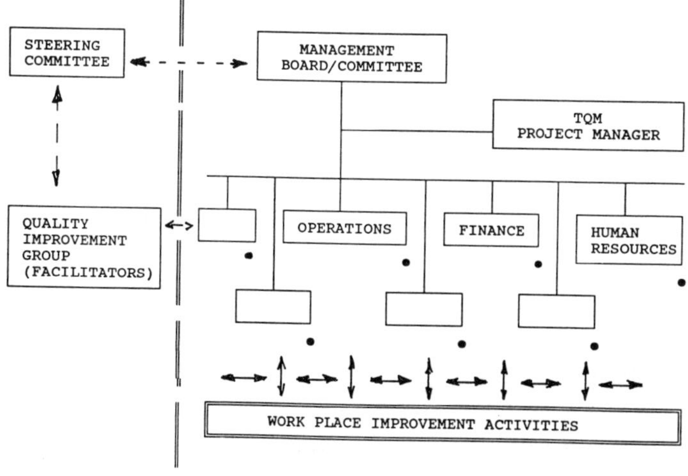

• = *facilitator*

The actual approach will be dependent upon the size of the organisation. Generally the first step is to appoint a coordinator/Project Leader (sometimes called Director of Quality) who will be responsible for managing the improvement process. In many cases this is a full time responsibility and the person concerned should report directly to the Chief Executive.

The management team should agree to act as a steering committee to focus senior management's attention on the development and strategy of the detailed plans for the implementation.

Care should be taken not to create numerous permanent committees. Where appropriate, 'ad hoc' groups should be formed as and when necessary from within the organisation. However, each divisional group should appoint a facilitator who has responsibility for:

- assisting with the development of the overall quality plan; and
- facilitating the improvement process within their own department.

The facilitators, with the coordinator, should develop the detailed plan for the management steering committee.

The objective is to help the people at the 'front line' to eliminate hassle and to introduce improvement activities.

SYSTEMS

Many quality initiatives fail because the necessary tools and procedures are not in place at the beginning. The key process items which need to be developed are discussed below.

Measurement A simple attribute measurement chart should be designed so that everyone can introduce it to record when the process causes a non-conformance to take place.

Flow charting This should be used in conjunction with methods for analysis of individual work processes covering such items as inputs, outputs, suppliers, and customers requirements to determine the most effective way of working. These techniques highlight the areas where measurement should be applied, to determine whether the process is in control and meeting the requirements of the customer.

Corrective action system It is essential to have a system to handle problems which are preventing individuals from carrying out their work correctly. The basic steps include.

(i) definition of the problem;
(ii) immediate fix to ensure that the customer's requirements are met;
(iii) determination of root cause and it's elimination;
(iv) feed back to ensure that corrective action has eliminated the problem.

Recognition Individuals must be recognised for their contribution to the improvement process. There are many different approaches. Some companies use a suggestion scheme with monetary rewards. Others have high visibility awards, team presentations to senior management etc. Everyone likes to be recognised. One of the most effective ways is to say 'thank you'. Initially concentrate on the informal recognition before developing a formal system which should have input from all levels. Also, consider who should determine which individuals or groups should be recognised -peer selection or boss selection?

Do not under-estimate the effect on the group by seeing ideas, which have been proposed either individually or on a group basis, being implemented. Management must provide the resources for this to take place.

Communication and awareness An effective communication and awareness plan should be developed, to suit the environment of your organisation. Many times communication and awareness takes place by default, and rumours develop which have an adverse affect. Timing of communication and the manner in which it is carried out is vital to it's success.

Tools There have been many articles/books written on the use of tools. In the early stages, everyone should be trained in the application of brainstorming, cause and effect diagrams, histograms, flowcharting, process analysis, simple attribute measurement charting and pareto (80/20 rule). However, as the improvement process gathers momentum, the need to use other techniques becomes apparent. Examples include:

- Failure mode and effects analysis
- Quality functional deployment
- Statistical process control
- Design of experiments
- Poka-yoke

Each of these tools has a major contribution to make. However, do not underestimate the beneficial effects to be achieved by the use of simple tools. The initial quality plan should determine which techniques should be used and the training required.

Education It is essential that everyone in the organisation receives education and training in TQM. TQM is a process of moving towards total continuous improvement. The type of training will be dependent upon the individual's function within the organisation.

The education process must ensure that all aspects of the plan are incorporated within the education and training sessions. The training should include understanding *theory*, supported by *practical* application, which leads to *action* within the workplace.

The whole emphasis must be on achieving a change in behaviour at all levels to eliminate waste and continuously improve.

Typical topics which should be considered are:

- Need for quality improvement, both organisational and individual.
- Organisation's mission, principles and values, together with a common language derived from the quality definition and policy statements.
- Analysis of work process, including supplier/customer relationship and requirements.

This training must be structured to ensure that changes take place in the workplace and that it continues forever.

Provide support

Management must ensure that sufficient time and resources are provided to develop and implement the plan. In addition, at that stage, management has to ensure that the quality initiative provides the required results. What are the results? How is the success of the improvement process to be measured? This should include which key processes need to be improved and how the effectiveness of the improvement process itself will be evaluated.

It is interesting to note that, in addition to selecting a key process which affected patients, consultants and hospital staff, St. Helier NHS Trust are measuring the success of the improvement process by assessing:

- use of corrective action system;
- use of measurement charts;
- effectiveness of the education process;
- number of suggestions made and implemented;
- change in pattern of complaints; and
- change in General Practitioner's perception.

Implementation

Once the detailed plan for making total quality management happen has been developed, then it is necessary to put it into effect. This covers the following.

- Preparing the education materials and tools.
- Getting started by training individuals and getting them involved in analysing their own work process.
- Maintaining the impetus by reviewing whether the objectives of the plan have been met, and what further activities should be incorporated into the business plan. This process audit should be continued *forever*. The key to maintaining the impetus lies with the line management and supervisors. They are the people who have ownership of work processes by their direct contact with employees.

It is necessary to create management behaviour which recognises the need for continuous improvement. George Bush, President of the USA, has said 'The improvement of quality in products and the improvement of quality in service - these are National priorities as never before.' If this is true for the USA it applies equally to the UK. The importance which the USA attaches to quality is recognised by the fact that the President annually presents the Malcolm Baldrige* National Quality Award. The key concepts required by this award can be used as the basis for an evaluation of your own quality improvement process. The criteria include the following.

- Quality is defined by the customer.
- The senior leadership of businesses needs to create clear quality values and build the values into the way the company operates.
- Quality excellence derives from well-designed and well-executed systems and processes.
- Companies need to develop goals, as well as strategic and operational plans to achieve quality leadership.
- Shortening the response time of all operations and processes of the company needs to be part of the quality improvement effort.
- Operations and decisions of the company need to be based upon facts and data.
- All employees must be suitably trained and developed and involved in quality activities.
- Design quality and defect and error prevention should be major elements of the quality system.
- Companies need to communicate quality requirements to suppliers and work to elevate supplier quality performance.

In Japan, one thing which seems to come naturally is Kaizen. Kaizen is a concept which leads to the belief that process improvement will reduce variables, cost and other losses such as waste associated with inefficient systems. Kaizen should exist naturally and is achieved by training people to understand, applying the improvement tools described earlier. The difference between Western and Japanese management is shown in Fig. 10.2.

Fig. 10.2 The difference between Western and Japanese management styles

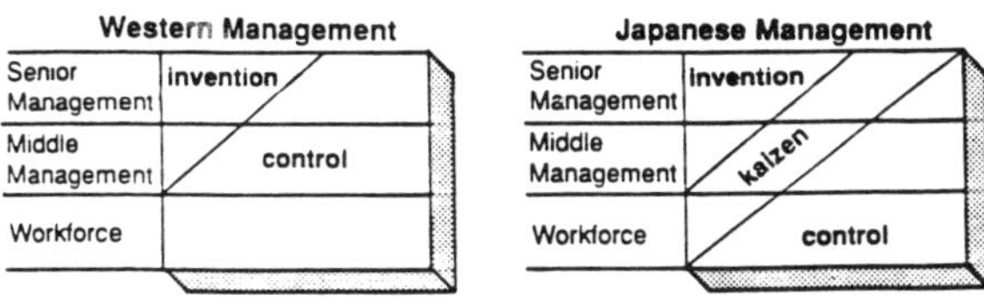

It can be seen that the Japanese use the word 'Kaizen' which simply means improvement. Kaizen does not replace the need for innovation. The two are complementary, yet independent, as shown in Fig. 10.3.

Fig. 10.3(a) Western management system as compared to (b) Japanese management system indicating the concept of Kaizen. Adapted from The Society of Motor Manufacturers and Traders Ltd (1991)

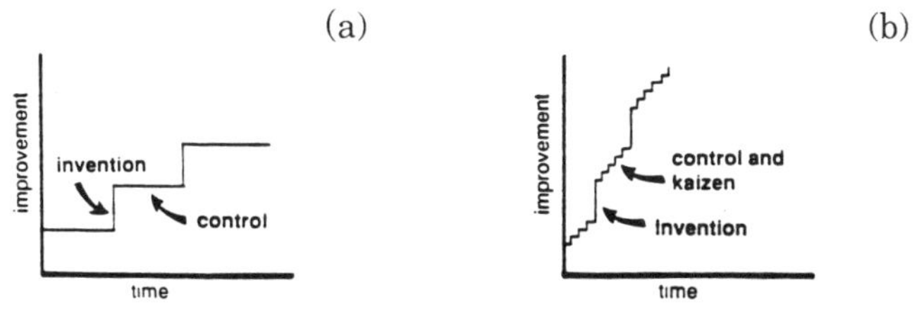

SUMMARY

Total Quality Management (TQM) is a process of achieving continuous improvement. This involves everyone in the organisation, and is forever. The aim is to eliminate waste, reduce variation in work processes and encourage innovation by employees, to ensure the maximum added value to the product or service provided.

The manufacturing industry in general has been referred to as it led the improvement process, followed by the service industry. Local Authorities and voluntary agencies in the social care sector are also beginning to look at the implications and advantages of TQM. The fact that the end product is 'care' rather than profit should not be used as an excuse to avoid the challenges of implementing TQM.

The elimination of waste and ensuring a greater say for the consumer in the management and quality of any service must be a primary focus for the quality conscious social care agency. Releasing the potential of staff and eliminating barriers to improvement are of no less value to a hard pressed Local Authority or voluntary agency than to a major successful industry.

To achieve this continuous improvement requires a management-led improvement process, which includes mission, principles, values, systems, tools, all of which are incorporated into an education/training programme to ensure that everyone knows what they have to do in the new environment. St. Helier NHS Trust summed this up as:

> We are seeking to create an environment in which management will lead staff rather than managing or supervising them. The potential of all our staff, led in the right direction, is enormous.

ACKNOWLEDGEMENTS

Many individuals and organisations have contributed to the development of the authors' ideas. However, with regard to this Chapter we would like to thank Bob Lawrie of the Society of Motor Manufacturers and Traders, and Nigel Sewell and Gerry Jenkins at St. Helier NHS Trust, Carshalton, for their help and assistance.

*The Malcolm Baldrige National Quality Award is managed by the United States Department of Commerce, Gaithersburg, MD 20899, USA and adminstered by the American Society for Quality Control, Milwaukee, WI 53201-3005, USA.

REFERENCES

Crosby, Philip, B. (1979). *Quality is Free.* McGraw Hill Book Company.

Crosby, Philip, B. (1984). *Quality Without Tears* . The Art of Hassle-Free Management. McGraw Hill Book Company.

Deming, W. Edwards (1986). *Out of the Crisis.* Cambridge University Press.

Herzberg, F. (1966). *Work and the Nature of Man.* Cleveland: World Publishing.

Ishikawa, Kaoru (1982). *Guide to Quality Control.* Asian Productivity Organisation.

Juran, J.M. (1988). *Juran on Planning for Quality.* The Free Press.

Macdonald, J., and Piggott, J. (1990). *Global Quality - The New Management Culture.* Mercury Books.

Maslow, A.H. (1943). A theory of human motivation. *Psychological Review,* 50.

Oakland, J.S. (1989).*Total Quality Management.* Oxford: Heinemann.

Peters, T.J. (1988). *Thriving on Chaos.* London: Macmillan.

Taylor, F.W. (1947). *Scientific Management - A Collection of Material* . Harper & Bros.

The Society of Motor Manufacturers and Traders (1991). *Tools and Techniques for Quality Management.* The Society of Motor Manufacturers and Traders Limited, London.

The authors would be pleased to discuss any points raised in this chapter. They can be contacted at Partners in Change Ltd, 9 Brackendale Grove, Harpenden, Herts AL5 3EL

11

The challenges of the quest for quality in social care services

Des Kelly and Bridget Warr

This introductory text has set out an overview of the main elements of quality in social care. It is argued that developing a structure and consideration of quality within social care services can be regarded as a comparatively recent phenomenon. However the authors are aware that good practice existed long before the concerns for defining and articulating quality actually received the attention it has recently been accorded. Chapters have reflected the perspective of service-users, the role of training, the place of management and of monitoring. These aspects are not simply overlapping approaches to the development of an effective framework for quality assurance in social care. Rather, they represent the essential strands of an integrated pattern which need to be woven together. Of course the picture is made more complicated because demands and expectations of social care services have changed, and will continue to change as our understanding and appreciation of standards develop. The creation of a market economy for social care provision is expected to add ever greater significance to the responsiveness of service providers.

THERE CAN be no doubt that quality is firmly on the agenda for the development of social care services in the 1990s. The challenges of change are wide ranging and far reaching: social and legislative, structural and organisational, managerial and consumerist. The way in which such change is likely to impact upon the planning, management and delivery of social care services for all user groups has been a major focus of this book. However, to some extent, all the contributors are seeking to hit a rapidly moving target. In the midst of the uncertainty which major change has heralded, quality has come to represent a 'back to basics' rallying point for better social care services.

There are several differing ideological viewpoints which have given rise to different approaches, all of which borrow concepts of quality from the commercial and business world and assert their relevance and application within welfare services such as social care. A critical account of such approaches, their limitations and potential actually to undermine good quality services is provided by Pfeffer and Coote (1991). They argue that the restructuring of welfare services along quasi-commercial lines has resulted in the emergence of four broad approaches:

- the traditional approach, to convey prestige and positional advantage
- the 'scientific' or expert approach, to meet standards set by experts
- the managerial or 'excellence' approach, to measure customer satisfaction
- the consumerist approach, to make the customer more powerful.

Pfeffer and Coote (1991) suggest that a failure to address fundamental differences between the services of commerce and welfare ultimately limits transferability and impact. Instead they suggest the strategy of a 'democratic approach', which utilises and adapts concepts from other approaches and is characterised by:

- equity;
- responsiveness; and
- empowerment.

It could be argued that there is no monopoly of good ideas by one perspective or political persuasion over another. However so much of what happens at the point of service delivery (in other words, where personal care needs are met by Care Assistants, Home Carers, Day Centre or Residential Workers, whatever the setting or the particular needs of the service-user), may seem to be a world away from theoretical considerations of constructs or models or policy. All sorts of rationalisations may be used to explain the gulf between rhetoric and reality. The way in which managers 'pick and mix' ideas and approaches will ultimately shape the context in which direct care services are provided. It is not the simple adapting and presentation of these ideas which create change, rather it requires conviction and commitment, enthusiasm and responsiveness. The writings of Peters (Peters and Waterman, 1982; Peters, 1987), a major proponent of the 'excellence' approach to management, indicate that the successful implementation of change requires a systematic programme; the words are easy but they are 'tough to execute'. Between the ideas which inspire and the structures which shape the services, there has to be emotional attachment by all involved to the principles of quality and quality assurance. This is made more difficult because often there has been a lack of appreciation of different understandings, interpretation and ways of working. There are three aspects of quality in social care services which, as yet, have been insufficiently acknowledged and as a result may have hindered developments.

- Quality is subjective
- Quality is relative
- Quality is perceptual

These three elements of quality in social care services need to be properly understood from the user perspective, through their involvement in providing feedback and evaluation about satisfaction and worth if positive and empowering services are ultimately to be offered.

The subjective, relative and perceptual aspects of quality are such that they have a powerful influence over the way in which social care services are seen to meet, or fail to meet, individual needs. They have to be placed in the context of sources of information including choice, alternatives and expectations. They are clearly shaped by and have the potential to shape current and future service arrangements.

A clearer understanding is required of the ways in which the subjective, relative and perceptual aspects of quality in social care can be integrated with the writings which emphasise, for example, accessibility, effectiveness, equality (Maxwell, 1984) or appropriateness, efficiency, equity (Shaw, 1986). The multidimensional characteristics of quality can thus begin to be described in ways which define it in the specific service or setting in which it is provided.

A particular challenge for social care in the midst of rapid change is to reconcile the broad underpinning values with the individualised notions of quality for service-users, alongside the necessary attitudinal changes for service providers and managers.

TRACING THE INFLUENCES FOR NEW WAYS OF WORKING

The Government White Papers, *Working for Patients* and *Caring for People* (DoH, 1989) set out a framework for health and social care provision which herald a radical shift in attitudes, and, in turn, the need to rethink approaches to service planning and provision. The proposed restructuring can be seen as a reaction to the catalogue of difficulties identified by the Audit Commission reports (1985, 1986) which led to the Griffiths' Report *Community Care: An Agenda for Action* (DoH & DSS, 1988) The underlying problems identified by such reports included:

- an inability of domiciliary services to keep pace with demographic trends;
- the rapid growth of private residential services inhibiting the development of more flexible forms of community care;
- considerable variation in service provision, and in

spending, between local authorities;

- uneven distribution of services and an inability to respond to user needs;
- organisational confusion especially between health authorities; social security and social services departments; and
- insufficient use of the informal networks of family and friends of service-users.

In addition there have been a series of well publicised cases of neglect and ill treatment towards vulnerable users, notably in residential settings.

The Griffiths report offered structural and funding solutions for a mixed economy of welfare, and this has been translated into legislative changes which separate the roles of purchaser and provider of community care services.

The array of writings which have followed the White Paper *Caring for People* and the subsequent guidance have been described as the development of a 'new language of welfare'. This new language is perhaps best represented by the management thinking which has fused the broad approaches of 'culture, quality and excellence'. It was particularly the management theory of excellence which caught the imagination and this can be evidenced in the impact of this approach within the personal social services. Peters and Waterman published *In Search of Excellence* in the USA in 1982. This book has been credited as beginning a new management movement which put customer care at the centre of service delivery. Peters and Waterman studied the most successful companies in the USA and sought to identify the reasons for their success. They describe practices in which the simple things are done well and use these to demonstrate the essential management attributes for successful performance, whatever the product or service. A British study by D. Clutterbuck published as *The Winning Streak* (Goldsmith and Clutterbuck, 1984) places greater emphasis on the calibre of leadership as the key characteristic of the best companies. This notion is also developed by Peters and Austin (1985) in *A Passion for Excellence* which sought to apply the principles of excellence to service industry.

The three key concerns identified are:

- care of customers;
- valuing the workforce;
- encouraging innovation.

These themes have clear parallels with the emergence of approaches to change in social care.

RESTATING DEFINITIONS

The efforts to develop a satisfactory definition for quality in social care have resulted in the emergence of a new vocabulary or 'quality babble'. As with any professional jargon it can prove unhelpful. Chapter 1 argued that common definitions in the workplace are required to improve communication and understanding.

Contributors have referred to the dictionary definitions which often equate quality with excellence. Both Gibbs and Sinclair (Chapter 6) on quality and inspection, and Richards (Chapter 9) in discussing concepts of quality and the North American influence draw on the paradigm of 'structure', 'process' and 'outcomes' developed by Donabedian as a way of broadening the understanding of quality in social care. Such an approach offers a useful framework although it appears to have received greater consideration within health care than within social care.

Garvin's (1984) multi-definitional approach to quality outlined by Dunnachie in Chapter 2 offers a well rounded view which usually illuminates applications in the complexity of social care services.

James argues in Chapter 3 that 'Quality is simply a social construct with a meaning attached to it'. She suggests that, for managers in the social services, the concept of quality has been a timely device in managing social care services in a period of rapid change. As such it has been a substitute for the core values which form a rallying point for practitioners. James also highlights the tensions inherent in the use of quality as a basis for managing services in social care.

It appears that within the social services, in its broadest

sense, more effort has been placed on defining quality in relation to social care than other aspects of service. Thus the thrust of the quality control aspects of the legislation has been directed towards residential services in particular. The standardising approach of the National Vocation Qualifications system have similarly targeted residential, domiciliary and day care work.

FROM VALUES TO VARIABLES FOR QUALITY

Concerns about the wide variation in standards of care services across the range of social care settings and sectors has been the major impetus for improvement.

There are many examples which could be cited. Typically they have been presented as the lack of consistency in the expectations or demands of the regulatory systems as applied from one sector to another or between different regulatory authorities.

The introduction of independent Inspection Units as part of the initial phase of community care legislation, discussed by Wing in Chapter 5, is intended, in part, to address these concerns.

A common theme to be observed across studies which have criticised the regulatory system is that of an apparent lack of any concrete definition of standards and thus inconsistencies and inflexibility in the ways in which judgements about quality have been made. It is clear that, as outlined by Ritchie in Chapter 4, establishing standards, setting and maintaining, as well as monitoring to safeguard standards are all important early stages to assuring quality in the delivery of social care services.

However there are a considerable number of questions which have to be answered along the way, including: Whose standards? Who defines? How do we ensure 'ownership' by all the stakeholders? At what level should standards be set? Ritchie suggests one approach to the setting and using of standards in social care services, others are being explored and a flow of writing on this subject can be anticipated over the next few years.

Statements on standards which have begun to influence

social care services have drawn on the importance of the value-base. The work of the Social Services Inspectorate in the *Caring for Quality* series has resulted in several publications relating to residential services which have used this approach. In *Homes are for Living in* (DoH & SSI, 1989) which is also referred by Gibbs and Sinclair (Chapter 6), the source for the values statements are the principles for good practice set out in *Home Life: A Code of Practice for Residential Care* (Centre for Policy on Ageing, 1984) namely

- independence;
- dignity;
- respect;
- choice;
- privacy; and
- fulfilment.

These concepts capture the fundamental values considered to be at the core of social care provision - the extent to which their interpretation characterises the relationships between the provider and recipient of care services will determine the perception of quality. It is this value-base as the cornerstone of social care which should differentiate the services of social care agencies from the straight commercial and business sector transactions. It seeks to acknowledge that the analogy of social care service users as 'customers' has to be in a somewhat different sense to which the term is usually applied.

Pfeffer and Coote (1991) argue that this requires customers to also be seen as citizens, and a strategy which ensures empowerment through rights, participation and different management arrangements. The same views are expressed in *Community Life: A Code of Practice for Community Care* (Centre for Policy on Ageing, 1990), which was compiled to compliment *Home Life: A Code of Practice for Residential Care* (Centre for Policy on Ageing, 1984), a significant benchmark for standards in residential provision. The concept of 'customers' of social care services is a complex one. There may be a tension between the interests of the direct users of services and their carers or parents. This raises questions in some peoples' minds about who is the customer? This may be more complicated when the voluntary and private sector are considered, since a common definition of 'customer' is the person who pays - in this setting it is more often local authorities than service users.

The equity, responsiveness, empowerment concepts used by Pfeffer and Coote (1991), offer a quality assurance framework for fitness of purpose and certain standards which again draws on values. Pfeffer and Coote summarise a set of principles, outlined below, which are fundamental to quality in social care.

Appropriate That assessment shows the service is what the individual or community actually need; assessment and reassessment procedures are clear and consistent.
Equitable That a fair process of distribution is seen to be working.
Participative That service-users should have the opportunity to influence decisions and the nature of services provided to them; the exercise of choice and right to self-determination are protected.
Accessible That the design, provision and control of services are accessible and as such not compromised by difficulties such as lack of information or the constraints of time and distance.
Acceptable That the services are provided to satisfy the expectations of users and other stakeholders; the right to respect and dignity are upheld.
Efficient That resources are used to maximum effect to benefit the users and other stakeholders.
Integrated That services are planned and coordinated with those provided by other agencies, public, private and voluntary.
Responsive That services are flexible enough to respond to the unique needs of the individual user and stakeholder.
Effective That services achieve the intended benefit for user and stakeholder; information should be available on the processes of monitoring, evaluation and inspection so that feedback to suggest improvements can be incorporated.

These variables can be regarded as the beginnings of a

framework for operationalising the values which underpin social care services. They provide a basis for negotiating individualised services capable of meeting assessed need within a context of consumer determined criteria for quality.

DEVISING MODELS AND METHODS FOR MEASUREMENT

In order to ensure quality it is necessary to have agreed means of measurement. The lack of agreement on standards combined with a lack of precision in the use of terms such as 'quality of care' and 'quality of life' have contributed to the delay in the proper consideration of the impact on the development of social care services. The publication of the White Paper *Caring for People* (DoH & DSS, 1989) and the subsequent Policy Guidance and the series of SSI materials on the quality theme have usefully stimulated debates within social care and across the points of contact with other agencies such as health, housing and education.

The setting of standards is an important process in defining the specific terms of quality in social care services. Agreed standards provide a reference point for services which can be used by all stakeholders. In addition they offer a basis for monitoring and evaluation as part of the quality assurance system.

The emergence of measures to determine quality in social care services remains at an early stage of development.

The Social Services Inspectorate Guidance on Standards documents and the publication of *Inspecting for Quality: Principles, Issues and Recommendations* (DoH, 1991) set out clearly the principles and preconditions for social care practice within an integrated system for quality assurance and these are referred to by Wing, Chapter 5, on inspection and evaluation. These are important first steps, they are the building blocks for future development. They begin to set out the infrastructure within which new service arrangements will be delivered.

Davis in an unpublished report on training for inspection staff prepared for the *Central Council for Education and Training in Social Work* (CCETSW) (Davis, 1992) argues that the absence of 'acceptable, national, outcome standards' will continue to be a problem. She refers in particular to the difficulties of the demands for evenhandedness, fairness and accuracy by inspectors reporting on residential homes. However she draws on the development of systems of 'outcome standards' in Nursing Homes used in Australia and the USA as examples of a beneficial approach.

A similar method has been proposed for setting standards within The Spastics Society with a focus on inputs, processes, outputs and outcomes. This is illustrated in Figure 11.1.

Fig. 11.1 The system for setting standards within the Spastic Society

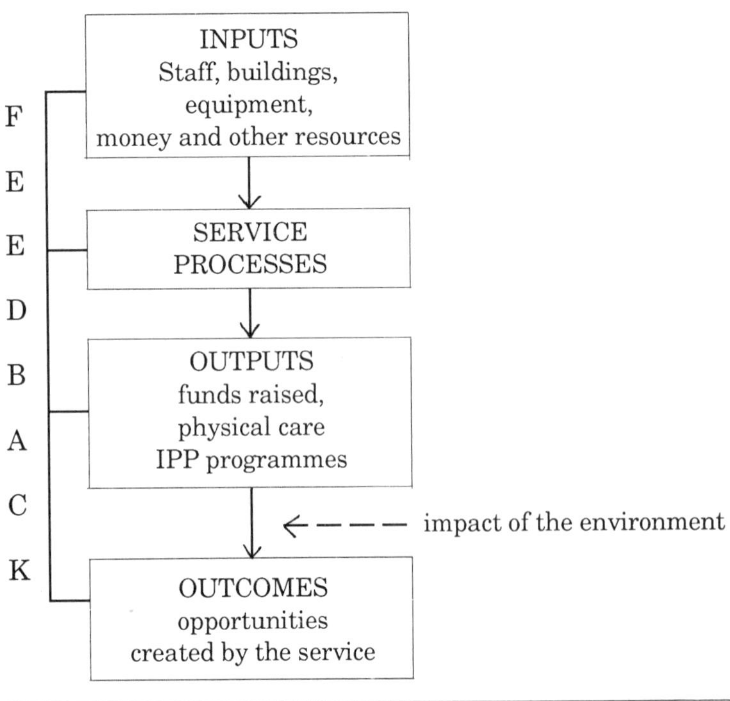

Clarifying the standards allows for critical review and evaluation, and comparisons between and across services.

There is still no commonly agreed definition of 'outcomes' as opposed to 'outputs': some would argue that the outcome of good care in the community sense is a service user who is independent, content and has strong links in the local community and beyond. Others would consider that to be too distant from the service provision and would consider outcome to be the opportunities which the service provides for the user (who may or may not wish to take full advantage of them). This debate has a long way to go before a clear and definitive explanation of the terms is agreed, but every attempt should be made to reach that point to facilitate progress.

Several models and methods to the measurement of quality have been outlined in earlier chapters. They serve to highlight the importance of synthesising both the 'quantitative' and 'qualitative' aspects of quality. Quantitative characteristics may be easier as has been evidenced by the regulation of residential services under the Registered Homes Act 1984 and the application of 'Home Life' (Centre for Policy on Ageing, 1984) as a code of practice. Many stories are told about the over-use of tape measures to make judgements about quality. The Audit Commission work has been successful in elucidating and incorporating quantitative aspects as a measure for social care services. Obvious examples are the numbers of carers and the numbers of hours deployed in home care; the number of attenders; the number of sessions and the user to staff ratio in a Day Care establishment; the total number of meals provided by a mobile meals service; fuel; and grocery costs; and so on. Such data provides comparative information which can be used to measure performance by individual service units as well as within and across agencies and services. Qualitative aspects are frequently referred to as 'soft' information, they include subjective criteria which are considered more difficult to evaluate. Examples may include the reputation of a residential unit; the enthusiasm, commitment and flexibility of a group of home carers; judgements about comfort or meaningful participation or trust in relationships.

The measures drawn on by Gibbs and Sinclair in their

checklist study (Chapter 6), namely *Homes Are for Living In* (DoH & SSI, 1989) and the material devised by Bradshaw represents attempts to objectify the qualitative data. The use of checklists are thus offered as a means by which attention can be directed to areas otherwise missed in the inspection process and, in particular, provides a useful aide memoire.

It could be argued that the ideological battles which resulted in the proposals for a 'mixed economy of welfare' have been won. The concept of 'enabling' as the primary purpose and responsibility of social care agencies has been incorporated into the preparation for planning and delivery and monitoring of services. The philosophical split between the notion of purchaser and provider has been achieved. The rhetoric has done its job and awaits the testing of reality. There can be no denying the need to be able to combine the quantitative and qualitative indicators in complementary ways to make judgements and set targets in social care is a fundamental strategic imperative.

Beck differentiates these quantitative and qualitative aspects of the inspection process as the 'science' and 'art' of inspection (Beck, 1991). She suggests the science 'is about the easily measurable, the quantifiable, the countable'.' This is where the tape measure and temperature chart come out, when you count toilets, people scrutinise staff hours and duty rotas. . . The art of inspection is in seeking one thing, being able to draw conclusions about another and in knowing how to test that conclusion'. Beck goes on to develop the idea that determining quality, making judgements and testing them out is something which is undertaken alongside other aspects of the inspection task. She describes the most valuable skill for inspectors as that of 'listening' in an active way and there are parallels with Wing's description of the evaluation process (Chapter 5).

There are also overlaps in this notion with Gibbs and Sinclair's reference to 'thoroughness' (Chapter 6), although interestingly their analysis reveals that high involvement in a particular method of gathering evidence for different inspectors does not necessarily lead to greater agreement in the overall evaluation.

In addition the need to put together a 'toolbox' of approaches to measuring quality in social care requires an understanding of the transitional context of service development. James (Chapter 3) refers to quality as a way of managing change and innovation; such change has a number of characteristics and dimensions including flexibility, innovation and decentralised models of working. This undoubtedly adds to the complexity that is social care. Practitioners and managers who wish to make use of quality concepts to develop social care services desire accessible systems which can be seen to get results. Being able to use the language of quality is worth nothing if it cannot be operationalised to directly effect the quality of care and the quality of life of service users.

NEW SKILLS FOR NEW WAYS OF WORKING

The development of measures to capture quality in social care services arise out of policy initiatives which herald new approaches to the planning, organisation and delivery of services. New structures and new ways of working are predicted, and new skills are likely to be necessary. Biggs and Weinstein (1991) suggest that the knowledge and competences relating to community care at qualifying levels share many familiar core skills across assessment, care management and inspection. They acknowledge that new skills will be necessary and these are likely to be important challenges for future social care service. Amongst the new themes identified are:

- relationships in a mixed welfare economy;
- an understanding of the merits and contribution of the independent sector at a local level;
- identifying standards and making judgements which include user views;
- service specification and congruence;
- contracting and negotiating with service providers and users;
- planning and working with users and informal carers;
- finance management; and

- notions of quality assurance achieved through monitoring and evaluation.

Quality assurance may be described as a new label which, to differing extents, is relevant to each of these 'new' aspects of service management and delivery. The challenges which are implicit in the rhetoric which has ushered in these changes are substantial and perhaps easy to underestimate. The demand for social care services which demonstrate genuinely *anti-discriminatory approaches* in the widest sense have been acknowledged by CCETSW to require 'considerable remedial training' (Biggs and Weinstein, 1991). The development of models to enable *user empowerment* , participation and advocacy similarly demand new relationships and enabling partnerships. Flexibility and *multidisciplinary* aspects to purchasing and providing social care services will also require changes in attitudes and different ways of working. Quality assurance is an overarching concept to these components. It is evident that quality cannot be regarded as an optional extra. The notion of quality through quality assurance and quality control has to be fundamental to the way in which services are planned, promoted and provided. In addition, monitoring to review and evaluate services, will similarly draw on the involvement and participation of all stakeholders to ensure quality remains responsive.

A further component to quality in social care services is that of staff development. It should be implicit in responding to new demands that refining skills and competence will require attention to the development and training needs of the workforce in social care. In Chapter 7 Clough has outlined the interrelated aspects of training and quality and the importance of a regular appraisal of training needs.

A quality assurance approach can have clear benefits for workers including:

- appropriate leadership and management;
- greater clarity of purpose for work;
- enhanced job satisfaction;
- more accurate targeting of service delivery;
- clearer understanding for workers of their contribution

to services; and

- an improved framework for staff development, training and supervision.

This is undoubtedly a similar message to that of the proponents of 'excellence in management', namely that valuing the workforce is central to ensuring quality service delivery. It is useful to be reminded:

> Staff who are not treated fairly and with respect cannot be expected to deliver high quality services to users. If those who work in community care are underpaid, undervalued and unorganised, they are unlikely to play a positive role in improving and maintaining quality of care. There is clear evidence that quality is improved if workers feel they are properly valued, and if they have some control, individually and collectively, over how their work is controlled.
>
> (COHSE, 1990)

Piggott and Piggott (Chapter 10) also reflect on the importance of involving workers fully in detailing the experience of implementing a system of Total Quality Management. It is clear that one of the messages of practising what quality assurance principles actually preach, is that successful change requires full involvement to turn perceived threats into positive opportunities.

Commitment to quality will require a procedure for self-evaluation by individuals and groups or teams in the range of work settings of social care. Alongside the rudimentary stage of development of measures accurately to assess quality in social care, self-evaluation formats have emerged in an ad-hoc way. Although generally acknowledged to be important they have yet to be adequately integrated into the mainstream of quality assurance systems, as outlined by Dunnachie in Chapter 2:

- user led services;
- valuing people;
- commitment and ownership of the idea of quality throughout the agency;

- clear aims and objectives;
- service design, planning and procedures;
- systems for monitoring and review of performance;
- effective communication;
- agreed and accepted standards;
- supervision, development and training for staff; and
- clear roles and responsibilities especially between managers and inspectors.

Ultimately, quality in the provision and delivery of good social care services demands the incorporation of all these attributes. It also requires that managers, practitioners and stakeholders at the unit level have given consideration to the ways in which they can periodically review progress to meeting the stated aims and objectives. One approach is by the use of an *annual review procedure* which records issues arising out of service delivery in ways which allow for previous responses to be described and evaluated, as well as anticipating the need for a proactive approach to the future. Such a self-evaluation technique for any social care services could include a review of the following areas:

- the extent to which aims and objectives are fulfilled;
- user and carer views on the quality of care;
- characteristics of the service including: information, flexibility, respect, participation opportunities;
- the physical environment or facilities provided;
- community involvement and integration;
- care planning and review;
- recording;
- staff training; and
- monitoring and inspection.

The development of quality systems necessitates the bringing together of processes and techniques from both within and outside the specific service. Self-evaluation will ideally be matched by external evaluation. There is an inherent tension between the responsibility to inspect and assure quality on the one hand, and offer guidance and support for development on the other. Wing (Chapter 5) offers an account, based on her own experience, of the ways in which relationships are important to establishing credibility and should be used in the context of a clear and consistent framework for measuring and assessing performance. Regulatory systems are only one approach to quality assurance.

Oakland (1990), in discussing Total Quality Management, suggests that there is nothing as inevitable as an idea whose time has come. Arguably the concept of quality assurance in social care is in just this position; Oakland goes on that 'there is also nothing as inevitable as the rejection of ideas that do not fulfil their promise'. Such is the challenge for social care services in the 1990s.

REFERENCES

Audit Commission (1985). *Managing Social Services for the Elderly More Effectively.* London: HMSO.

Audit Commission (1986). *Making a Reality of Community Care.* London: HMSO.

Beck, J. (1991). Measure for measure. *Social Work Today*, 30 May, p.22.

Biggs, S. and Weinstein, J. (1991). *Assessment, Care Management and Inspection in Community Care: Towards a Practice Curriculum.* London: CCETSW.

Centre for Policy on Ageing (1984). *Home Life: A Code of Practice for Residential Care.* London: CPA.

Centre for Policy on Ageing (1990). *Community Life: A Code of Practice for Community Care.* London: CPA.

COHSE (1990). *Evidence to House of Commons Social Services Committee. 7th Report on Community Care.*

Davis, A. (1992). *Registration, Inspection and Quality Control.* (unpublished report for CCETSW).

Department of Health (1990). *Care Management and Assessment: Practitioners Notes.* London: HMSO.

Department of Health (1990). *Guidance on Standards for Residential Homes for Elderly People.* London: HMSO.

Department of Health (1990). *Implementing Community Care: Purchaser, Commissioner and Provider Roles.* London: HMSO.

Department of Health (1991). *Inspecting for Quality: Principles, Issues and Recommendations.* London: HMSO.

Department of Health (1991). *The Right to Complain.* London: HMSO.

Department of Health & Department of Social Security (1988). *Community Care: An Agenda for Action.* Chair, R. Griffiths. London: HMSO.

Department of Health & Department of Social Security (1989). *Caring for People: Community Care in the Next Decade and Beyond.* Cmnd 849. London: HMSO.

Department of Health & Social Services Inspectorate (1989). *Homes are for Living In.* London: HMSO.

Garvin, D. A. (1984). What does product quality really mean? *Sloan Management Review,* Autumn.

Goldsmith, W. and Clutterbuck, D. (1984). *The Winning Streak.* London: Weidenfeld and Nicolson.

Kelly, D. (1988). Maximising quality in the residential environment. *Social Work Today*, 4 March, pp.21-25.

Maxwell, R. J. (1984). Quality measurement in health. *British Medical Journal*, 288.

Oakland, J. S. (1990). *Total Quality Management: A Practical Approach*. London: DTI.

Peters, T. J. and Waterman R. H. (1982). *In Search of Excellence: Lessons from America's Best-Run Companies.* New York: Harper and Row.

Peters, T. J. and Austin, N. (1985). *A Passion for Excellence: The Leadership Difference.* Collins.

Peters, T. J. (1987). *Thriving on Chaos.* Macmillan.

Pfeffer, N. and Coote, A. (1991). *Is Quality Good for You?* A Critical Review of Quality Assurance in Welfare Services, 1PPR Paper 5.

Shaw, C. D. (1986). *Introducing Quality Assurance.* Kings Fund Project No.64.

Notes on contributors

Ian Baillie is Director of Social Work, Church of Scotland Board of Social Responsibility. He Chairs the Wagner Development Sub-Group on Aspects of Quality in Residential Care which has been concerned with quality issues in relation to residential services.

Roger Clough is Chief Inspector with Cumbria Social Services Department. He was Senior Lecturer in Social Work at the University of Bristol from 1978 to 1990, where he promoted a special interest in residential work. He has written several books and many articles on work in residential settings. His most recent book is *Practice, Politics and Power in Social Services Departments* (1990) published by Gower.

Mike Devenney is Managing Director of Changing Image, a disability consultancy. He has cerebral palsy with a speech impairment. Following work in the voluntary sector and with local authorities he became an Assistant Chief Officer at the London Borough of Ealing. He has been a Labour Councillor for Islington since 1986 and Chaired the Social Services Committee from 1988 to 1991. He has lectured extensively on disability and social services issues including in New Zealand and USA.

Hugh Dunnachie is Head of Quality Assurance for the Royal County of Berkshire Social Services Department.

Ian Gibbs is Research Fellow at the Centre for Housing Policy at the University of York.

Ann James is Fellow in Human Service Organisations at the Kings fund College and Honorary Senior Lecturer in Social Services Management at the University of Birmingham. She created the postgraduate open learning programme for mid career managers in her capacity as the first Director of the Social Services Management Unit at the University of Birmingham. In 1988 she wrote *Managing to Care* which was a DoH/SSI report based on inspection of management in statutory social services. She has recently completed a study, *Committed to Quality,* commissioned and funded by DoH/SSI which has focused on organisational or systemic change arising out of the Community Care Act and Children Act.

Des Kelly is Deputy General Secretary of the Social Care Association and manages the Social Care Practice Centre within a joint SCA (Education) and National Institute for Social Work staff development centre at the University of Warwick, Science Park. He was Head of Home of a residential establishment for older people and has substantial experience of working in residential settings. He has acted as consultant and has contributed to many training courses in social care. He was a member of the Wagner Committee which produced *Residential Care: A Positive Choice* in 1988, and of the Project Group which led to the DoH/SSI Guidance, *Inspecting for Quality,* published in 1991. As a regular contributor to social work magazines he has written widely on social care issues.

Gillian Piggott is a qualified Human Resources professional and a member of the Institute of Personnel Management. Her experience has included all aspects of the personnel function within the Service Industry. She is an active member of her local branch of IPM, and acts as External Assessor for the IPM Certificate of Personnel Practice course, currently being held In-House by a nation-wide food retailer.

John B Piggott has been involved in quality and reliability since 1961. Following 27 years of quality experience with General Motors, he moved into consultancy in 1989 and joined Gilbert Associates (Europe) Ltd., in 1991. He is an authority in the quality field; he was Chairman of the Society of Motor Manufacturers and Traders Quality and Reliability Panel from 1980 to 1988; a member of the Institute of Manufacturing Engineers Quality Management Group. John Piggott is a Chartered Engineer, a member of the Institution of Mechanical Engineers, a member of the Institute of Manufacturing Engineers, a Fellow of the Institute of Quality Assurance and a Senior member of the American Society for Quality Control.

Huw Richards is a Social work Commissioner, Mental Welfare Commission for Scotland and Honorary Lecturer at the Centre for Community Mental Health in Europe at Goldsmiths College. He is co-author of a workbook on Quality in health and social care, *The Enquire System* published in 1990.

Pete Ritchie has been involved in developing models of quality assurance at the Norah Fry Research Centre at the University of Bristol. Since moving to Scotland he has been working independently with a range of organisations on issues concerning quality in community care. He is currently working with Key Housing in Glasgow to implement an agency wide system for quality in staffed housing.

Ian Sinclair is Professor of Social Work in the Department of Social Policy and Social Work at the University of York. He was formerly Director of Research at the National Institute for Social Work.

Bridget Warr is Director of Inspection and Quality Assurance for The Spastics Society. She was Principal Adoption and Fostering Officer with the London Borough of Ealing before moving to the British Agencies for Adoption and Fostering as Assistant Director.

Heather Wing is Head of Inspection and Registration, Surrey County Council Social Services Department. Her background includes management in a residential setting. She is Chairperson of the National Association of Inspection and Registration Officers.